TOMES
of TERROR

Haunted Bookstores and Libraries

With a foreword by John Robert Colombo

Mar⸍ 1 ⸍

D1501655

DUNDURN
TORONTO

Project Editor: Carrie Gleason
Editor: Jenny McWha
Design: Laura Boyle
Cover Design: Laura Boyle
Front Cover Image: © Dreamstime/Paul Sparks
Printer: Webcom

Library and Archives Canada Cataloguing in Publication

Leslie, Mark, 1969-, author
        Tomes of terror : haunted bookstores and libraries / Mark Leslie.

Issued in print and electronic formats.
978-1-4597-2860-8 (pbk.).--ISBN 978-1-4597-2861-5 (pdf).--
ISBN 978-1-4597-2862-2 (epub)

1. Haunted places. 2. Ghosts. 3. Libraries--Miscellanea.
4. Bookstores--Miscellanea. I. Title.

BF1471.L48 2014   133.1'22   C2014-904249-3
                                      C2014-904250-7

1 2 3 4 5   18 17 16 15 14

We acknowledge the support of the **Canada Council for the Arts** and the **Ontario Arts Council** for our publishing program. We also acknowledge the financial support of the **Government of Canada** through the **Canada Book Fund and Livres Canada Books**, and the **Government of Ontario** through the Ontario Book Publishing Tax Credit and the **Ontario Media Development Corporation**.

Care has been taken to trace the ownership of copyright material used in this book. The author and the publisher welcome any information enabling them to rectify any references or credits in subsequent editions.

J. Kirk Howard, President

The publisher is not responsible for websites or their content unless they are owned by the publisher.

Printed and bound in Canada.

Visit us at
Dundurn.com | @dundurnpress | Facebook.com/dundurnpress | Pinterest.com/dundurnpress

Dundurn
3 Church Street, Suite 500
Toronto, Ontario, Canada
M5E 1M2

To Ron Roberts and all the good folks who worked at Levack Public Library, one of the first places where I discovered the wonder and magic that books bring into people's lives

And to librarians and booksellers everywhere — thanks for your advocacy in consistently offering up infinite power to the thirsty minds of the world.

"A room without books is like a body without a soul."

— *Cicero*

CONTENTS

Foreword: In for a Surprise! by John Robert Colombo.............12

Preface: My Life-Long Love Affair with Books, Writing, and
Things That Go Bump in the Night..15

Acknowledgements 20

CANADA 23
    The Mischievous Bookseller's Elves...24
    The Eerie Elevator 27
    The Hitchhiking Ghost..31
    Haunted Country Bookshop 33
    The Runnymede Ghost..35
    Ghosts in the Attic 39
    Spirits of the Poorhouse Wretched 42
    The Rocking Chair Ghost 45
    Haunted History Books..51
    Inuit Carving Display Mystery..55
    Go Toward the Light!...59
    The Shadowy Figure 62

Spectres in the Stacks..65

The Miraculous Survival of the Parliamentary Library 68

Goosebumps at Smithbooks.....................................71

UNITED STATES OF AMERICA...............................74

Kerouac's Favourite Haunt.....................................76

The Tragic Story of Young Molly 81

The Portal..84

The Haunted Poetry Book 88

Death and Resurrection of The Book House.............91

Some Browse Forever 95

The Grieving Ghost of Greene's 98

Reading in the Dark... 100

Nat the National Treasure 103

The Ghost of Harriet Haskell................................. 106

Spellbinding Stories 111

The Many Lives of Carnegie Library 113

Smile, You're On Ghost Camera! 118

All Ghosts Want Some Peace of Mind 125

A Ghost Called Lola... 127

The Ghost of Doctor Harris................................... 131

When I Die, I'll Leave You My Books and My Ghost 143

The Curse of Old Lady Gray.................................. 146

When a Ghost Calls Your Name 152

Not So Sweet When You Build on a Grave 156

The Dedicated Ghost of Ida Day............................ 161

A Rowdy, Hidden Presence 165

Millicent the Muse 169

Things That Go Ding in the Night.......................... 174

Have Ghosts, Will Travel....................................... 179

The Ghost with a Library Card............................... 181

INTERNATIONAL.. 187

Ghosts of the Royal Library.................................... 188

The White Lady of The Haunted Bookshop 191

Lord Combermere's Chair 193

Macabre Secrets of the Municipal Palace 197

Sternberg's Ghost 199

The Book-Loving Ghost of Felbrigg Hall 202

The Blue Man 205

Open To All 207

A Treasure of Infinite Haunts 209

The Hidden Note in Marsh's Library 211

Old Jacobus of Rammerscales 214

Ghost in a Dark Green Jacket 216

The Mysterious Book of Antiquities and Curiosities 217

The Nun in Blue 220

The Restless Librarian 222

When a Book Gets Under Your Skin 224

Afterword 227

Further Reading and Additional Resources
for the Bookish at Heart 229

Appendix A: Eberhart's List of Haunted Libraries 230

Appendix B: Recommended Reading 232

Appendix C: Bookseller Associations 250

Notes 252

FOREWORD

In for a Surprise

by John Robert Colombo

If you have yet to set eyes on Mark Leslie, the author of this engaging book, you are in for a surprise, maybe even a shock!

Mark is a man to mark (if I may be permitted a pun) — he is very tall, dynamic, personable, knowledgeable about books and the book trade, especially books about ghosts and spirits, and very enthusiastic about life in general (and, let me add, about the afterlife as well.)

The best description of him comes from an email that he sent to me not too long ago. It includes the following self-appraisal: "In a nutshell, I am an avid book lover and have been all of my life. I have always been fascinated by 'things that go bump in the night.' (And quite terrified of them — I consider myself one of the world's biggest chickens — I'm afraid of the dark, afraid of the monster under my bed, the one hiding under the stairs, etc.

As a parent, when my son said he thought the bogeyman was in his room, I used to hide under the covers with him and wait for my wife to come save us....) *Tomes of Terror* combines my two greatest loves — my love of books and storytelling with my love of spooky tales."

No one could have expressed it better, which is why I am quoting his own words here, but there is another reason: we are rather alike. I too love to read books and to write and compile them, and I too am fascinated with tales of the supernatural and theories of the paranormal. When those interests (or obsessions) mix and match, they generate more questions than they do answers, and many a great story of a haunting is born along the way!

Mark has honed his style as the compiler of two collections in the field of ghost-hunting: *Spooky Sudbury* (2013) and *Haunted Hamilton* (2012). They demonstrate that he has a special feel for locale, for he subscribes to the notion that it is places (like houses, residences, and public buildings) that are the scenes of hauntings. There is a lot of literature about haunted castles, and so on, to bear him out. My own position is that in most instances of reported hauntings, whether by ghosts or poltergeists, it is people rather than places who are haunted. This was also the position of George and Iris Owen, Canada's most widely respected "ghost hunters." Indeed, Iris was known to say, "Parapsychology is people." Without a person present there is no ghostly presence. Perhaps it takes a person and a place to raise a ghost.

I would like to think, along with Mark, that books attract spirits and that collections of books house covens of spirits. This being so, what a remarkable undertaking is *Tomes of Terror*, for it allows Mark to haunt (if I may use that word) more than fifty old and new bookstores, public libraries, and college and university libraries across Canada, the United States, the United Kingdom, and elsewhere, in search of accounts of ghost-like apparitions and poltergeist-like manifestations.

Here we enter into the realm of legend and tradition, folklore and urban lore, but we also enter into the domain of the personal experience of men and women who are now living. Strange events and experiences are either supernatural in nature (traditional stories or narratives) or paranormal in nature (accounts that may be described as memorates, that is, first-person recitals of what happened or what seemed to have happened.) Whatever their nature, they are, in essence, scary!

In the aisles of bookstores and the shelves and stacks of libraries, Mark has researched these supernatural stories, and he has interviewed those people who have been cursed, or blessed, with experiences of a paranormal nature. In doing so, he adds to our cache of experiences as human beings. Perhaps Mark will join me in affirming my maxim that "Ghosts are good for us." They are good for us because while they may frighten us, they require us to think in terms that extend beyond the quotidian — the everyday — and embrace such notes as life and death, fate and destiny, fear and hope, acceptance and affirmation, belief and doubt, and grace and deliverance.

Earlier, I mentioned that if you have not yet set eyes on Mark, you should be prepared for a shock. What I had in mind is what he shared with me in an email: the fact that Mark has a unique sidekick named Barnaby — a life-sized skeleton who travels with him on most of his book tours, spending a good deal of his time in the passenger seat of his car, and startling drivers all over Hamilton and Toronto. In the past couple of years, Barnaby has become a central part of Mark's persona as a writer of horror and the paranormal.

If you want to see Mark and his sidekick Barnaby Bones, visit the following website: *http://www.pinterest.com/markleslie/barnaby-bones/*.

But don't say I didn't warn you!

PREFACE

My Life-Long Love Affair with Books, Writing, and Things That Go Bump in the Night

I have had a life-long love affair with books. I have also never grown out of the special thrill that comes with telling and listening to creepy tales of the eerie and uncanny. Although the way in which I have enjoyed and embraced books in all their many wonderful formats has changed multiple times over the decades, my passion for books — as well as my passion for eerie tales — has never wavered.

A box in my mother's basement is filled with a plethora of books of various shapes and sizes that were read to me, which as a child I thumbed my way through, looking at the pictures, and eventually learned to read for myself. While one particular memory of being read to when I was young comes to me, I can definitely identify reading and book-related rituals from my childhood playing a significant role in me eventually defining myself as a "Book Nerd."

One such ritual was those special Tuesdays, when the periodical and comic book deliveries arrived at the Mini Mart in Levack, Ontario. My mom, who worked there part-time, would come home with a weekly surprise for me: two or three different comic books. In the early days it was Gold Key and Harvey and Charlton comics. Mixed in, occasionally, were creepy comic books like *The House of Mystery*, *Tales from the Crypt*, and *Ghosts*. I remember carefully turning those pages, frightened at the stories that were unfolding but unable to resist their special, creepy allure, particularly when hosts such as Cain or the Crypt Keeper beckoned me to keep reading.

Yet, even during the richest depths of my intense love for comic books, I branched out and learned to also love reading books. I began the journey through stories rich with mystery, such as *Hardy Boys* and *Encyclopedia Brown* and *Alfred Hitchcock and the Three Investigators*, as well as so many stand-alone novels that captured my imagination. The sense of unknown in these tales drew me in. I also recall loving various books about adventures in caves (I was fascinated with caves for the longest time — and why not, they were dark and creepy places), and stories written by Lester Del Rey and other sci-fi writers about adventures on the moon and on Mars. Over the years, I accumulated a number of books on the paranormal and unexplained phenomenon, further strengthening that life-long passion of mine: stories that scared and frightened me.

I grew up in a small mid-northern Ontario town called Onaping Falls. With a population somewhere in the realm of 6,000, Onaping Falls didn't have a bookstore. But it did have a library. One of the wonderful librarians who worked there seemed to have taken a liking to me — although I'm sure she was kind and generous of her time with any child who stepped through the door. She quickly learned my tastes in reading and picked up on my fascination with the paranormal, and eventually I would no sooner walk in the door and she would beam a smile and tell me about some new arrivals that she just knew I had to have.

"A new book on Sasquatch arrived this week, Mark," I remember her saying one time when I walked past the check-out desk. "I put it aside for you to have a look at." I think it might have been Ann Slate and Alan Berry's 1976 version of *Bigfoot*.

The United Church, another important edifice of my child-hood, always held great bazaars, which were a wonderful spot to get comics and mass market paperbacks. One book I remember reading and re-reading was called *Monsters Among Us: Journey to the Unexplained*, by John Lee and Barbara Moore. It was filled with tales about the strange and mysterious, including the Bermuda Triangle, Bigfoot, UFO spacemen, the Abominable Snowman, the Loch Ness Monster, and Easter Island. I was both captivated by the wondrous tales and terrified to turn out the lights at night.

My reading habits continued to migrate over the years and I always defined myself as a science-fiction reader, even though, for the most part, I was never into the "hard" sci-fi novels. My cup of tea, it seemed, was more akin to enjoying "weird fiction" or "Twilight Zone"-styled tales — stories that lie just off-centre from reality.

A love of writing that began while I spent the final days of my thirteenth year hammering away on my mom's Underwood typewriter is a passion that continues to grow. By the time I was finishing high school, the only thing I knew I wanted to do for sure was write. My parents, quite wise to the ways of the world, strongly advised that I would need to have a good job in order to support myself as a writer. Whenever there was a television program on about a writer, it usually showed them starving and eating nothing but Spam or Kraft Dinner, which Mom would point out to me. That was her way of reminding me that writers don't make a lot of money.

I was too bull-headed, though, and continued to pursue writing. I studied English Language and Literature at university, only to realize that there weren't many jobs suited for someone with my background — and that's when I landed a part-time job at Coles, a Canadian mall bookstore chain. And, although I had been bitten by the book bug already, the experience of working in a bookstore (which had been like a fantastical dream that was too good to be true) drove that sickness to a whole new level.

I wasn't just bitten by the book bug, I was bitten by a book-seller bug, too. Much like that wonderful librarian I remember who delighted in sharing the marvels of the new releases with patrons, I too learned the special thrill of what it means to understand my favourite core customers enough to truly and intuitively feel out just the right book for them. There is something magical about placing the perfect book in the proper customer's hands, and the feeling you get when that customer returns to talk about the reading experience they have had.

Like so many librarians and so many booksellers before me, I also understand that bookstores and libraries aren't just buildings used to store books. They are, of course, much more than the sum of their dusty old shelves. They are magical places, places where connections are made, where information and passions are shared. Bookstores and libraries are like shrines or temples to book lovers. We know that walking through the door is like stepping into a magical dimension where virtually anything can happen.

Tomes of Terror is, for me, the culmination of my greatest lifelong passions: my passion for writing, my passion for books, and my passion for sharing creepy and eerie tales. I had a fun time exploring these worlds and these stories, and I hope that you have just as much fun reading them.

As I finish the first draft of the book, somewhat saddened that this part of the journey is almost over, I am already wondering what other eerie bookish delights I might next explore. But I am getting ahead of myself....

Right now, there are countless aisles for you and I to walk down together, marvellous bookish locales around the world to explore. Sure, some of the stories will be a bit frightening, some of them might cause a cold shiver of terror to run down your spine, still others might make you smile or laugh, and others, ever sad, might inspire a tear.

Come, let's crack those covers together.

ACKNOWLEDGEMENTS

I'd like to thank my Mom for instilling the love of reading in me. It started with the weekly batch of comics she bought from the Mini Mart where she worked when I was young, and it developed into a lifelong passion for reading and for books.

Many thanks are due to the good folks at Dundurn, who have taken my words and made them into a book that is truly greater than the sum of its parts, from the words and notes, all the way through to the cover, layout, and design that make a product we can all truly be proud of. Thanks to Beth Bruder from Dundurn for not only believing in this project from the initial proposal, but for believing in me and the vision I had to write non-fiction paranormal books from the very beginning, when the spark for *Haunted Hamilton* was first born. Thanks also to Carrie Gleason for helping refine it into the balanced "love for books and love for spooks" it was meant to be, and to Jenny McWha and Laura Harris, who helped to carefully craft my words and these stories from good into great. The manner by which Dundurn's editorial team took my unbridled passion for books and ghosts and helped me to channel those elements into the book this became, is evidence of the fine work that editorial direction can bring to an author. I have adored seeing Margaret Bryant in action, selling and talking about my books to buyers, booksellers, and librarians; I am similarly thrilled when planning marketing strategies and execution with James Hatch and Karen McMullin.

I have long been a fan of John Robert Colombo's incredible compilations of ghost stories and am honoured to have him write such a fun foreword. John Robert Colombo is the author, editor, compiler, and translator of over 220 books. He has been called "Canada's Mr. Mystery" for such collections as the trilogy comprised of *Mysterious Canada* (1988), *Ghost Stories of Ontario* (1995), and *Haunted Toronto* (1996). His most recent title in this field is *Jeepers Creepers* (2013).

There are so many other folks — booksellers, librarians, and other writers and creators — who helped me, provided insight, made suggestions for stories, and allowed me access to information or photographs; they include Steve Vernon, Sophie Gorsky, Rob Evans, Gerard Miley, Aeryn Lynne, Sonia Roberts, Carolyn Longworth, Diane Macklin, Moe Hosseini-Ara, Kerrie Hughes, Diana Portwood, John Robbie, Meg Uttangi Matsos, Jan Maas, Lorraine Eastwood, Michelle Barron, Lorna Toolis, Greg Hage, and Shannon Hayes. I am certain that I missed at least a half dozen others, and so must throw out a blanket thank-you to my fellow authors and booksellers, and the kindred-spirited librarians who truly understand the intense and undying passion that propels book lovers into each new day.

The title for the book was inspired from a book review series of the same name that Steve Rapsky wrote for *The Gully Gazette*

(Levack District High School's newspaper), which I edited in 1987. Steve's passion for books, in particular horror novels, was quite contagious.

And, finally, thanks to Francine and Alexander, who allowed me the time away from those special family moments to dwell among the virtual stacks as I threw myself into this book. Your support and belief in me is a good part of what kept me going and allowed me to dance even when the muse wouldn't dance with me. I love you both with all of my heart, and I adore the "book" we have written together.

CANADA

THE MISCHIEVOUS BOOKSELLER'S ELVES

Gryphon Books

Edmonton, Alberta

When you walk into a store that has been securely locked overnight, you expect everything to be the way you left it. Unless, of course, there were unseen visitors flitting about, up to mischief, after you left the night before.

That's exactly what happened to the owner of Gryphon Books in Edmonton. Donna Tremblay (not her real name) believes her store was home to what she refers to as "mischievous bookworm elves."[1]

A few months into the store's operation, Tremblay, a former school teacher, was comfortable with the smooth operation. Running her own bookstore was a passion and a dream, one that she had methodically worked toward and planned for over the years. But when she unlocked the store one morning, she discovered books piled in stacks in various places throughout the store.[2] Not understanding what had happened, but still with a business to run, she re-sorted the books onto their appropriate shelves before opening the store for the day.[3]

When it kept happening, Tremblay began to notice a pattern. After several mornings of discovering piles of books, she detected that the books weren't just in random locations like she had first suspected. The piles tended to appear in two distinct locations: near the cash register and by the stairs leading to the basement.[4]

Instead of being worried or frightened by the inexplicable and eerie occurrences, Tremblay simply started arriving a bit earlier in order to have the time to tidy up the mess made by the unseen forces.[5] She treated the misplaced books no differently than if customers had walked in, grabbed books off of the shelves, and then set them down in another location — it was merely a side effect of running a bookstore.

It was only when she took to hanging "No Smoking" signs throughout the store that Tremblay had the chance to experiment with the spirit that walked, unseen, down her aisles. The first morning after she hung several of the signs, they were all on the floor, presumably having fallen off the walls during the night. Several days later, she found some of the signs as far as a dozen feet away from where they had originally hung, and one of them was even tucked away behind some shelved books.[6]

Tremblay began experimenting with the nightly sign-mover, and eventually determined that there was a single spot near the front of the store where she could hang the sign and have it remain undisturbed. So she abandoned the rest of the signs and stuck with the single one that stayed exactly where she placed it.[7]

She never did, however, find a similar solution for the misplaced books that continued to haunt her the entire time she owned and ran the bookstore. She merely got used to the nightly activity and cleaned up every morning. She discovered that the building the store was located in dated back to the 1800s and had been home to several other types of businesses over the years.[8] With a building that old, there was certainly a lot of history, and potentially a spirit that enjoyed moving the stock around in the dark of the night.

THE EERIE ELEVATOR

Waterdown Public Library
Dundas, Ontario

The mysterious occurrences at Waterdown Library began almost immediately after a new elevator was installed in 1978.

From the beginning, the elevator began taking unexplainable trips all on its own. Library staff and patrons reported seeing the elevator doors opening, despite nobody having called it, and the car taking unmanned trips back and forth between floors.

When library staff called the manufacturer of the elevator to get to the bottom of the malfunctioning install, the company reported that there was absolutely nothing wrong with either the mechanics or the wiring. Third party inspections confirmed the results.

But the elevator continued to operate as if guided by unseen patrons.

Speaking with the spouse of one of the previous librarians, I heard several tales of the elevator door opening and closing on its own and then going up for no detectable reason. One evening a group came to the library to take a display away and got caught between floors for a significant amount of time. Before the elevator resumed its course and set its prisoners free, panic set in and speculation arose that something truly unexplainable was going on.

One explanation for the cause of the disturbance comes from a pair of white marble tombstones that were found in 1978 and now hang beside the elevator with a plaque that reads:

> *These stones in memory of Waterdown's first settlers, Alexander Brown and his wife Merren Grierson, were placed here in 1979 when the interior of this building was reconstructed as a library.*
> *The Brown family had replaced them in the Union Cemetery, Waterdown, with one large tombstone on which Mrs. Brown's name appears in correct form. These were found quite by chance early in the year of celebrating the Centennial of Waterdown's Incorporation 1978–1979.*

Popular legend has it that the slight misspelling of Merren Grierson's name on the tombstone (spelled as Merion rather than Merren) might have something to do with the odd and unusual behaviour of the elevator.

Despite regular inspections into the elevator's activity, all revealing it to be in good working order, staff and visitors to the library continue to witness the elevator operating independent of human activity, the doors opening and closing for no good reason, and the occasional unexplainable sound of footsteps and voices when there is nobody else around.[9]

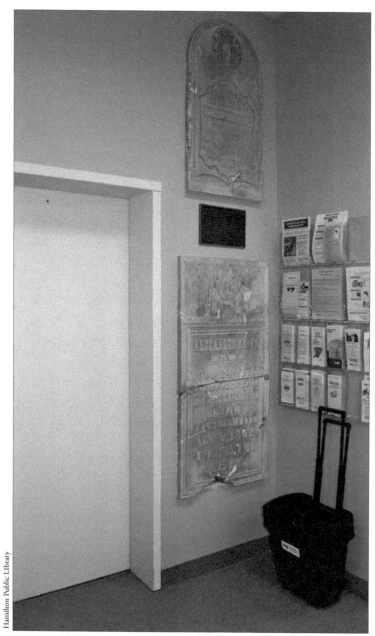

Elevator and tombstones at Waterdown Library

The library is slated to move to a new building in late 2014. The elevator will not be making the move, but the tombstones likely will. One wonders if the bizarre and unexplainable behaviour will move along with them. Of course, only time will tell.

First established in 1966, the Waterdown Branch of the Hamilton Public Library moved to its current location on Mill Street North, a designated building of Historical and Architectural value under the Ontario Heritage Act thirteen years later. Soon it will embark on yet another move to a 23,000-square-foot facility that will include the Waterdown Public Archive, multi-purpose recreational facilities, municipal services, community centre, and police services. The library will be located at 163 Dundas Street West at a significant elevation of the Niagara Escarpment, offering not only a picturesque view, but a unique and bold architecture that incorporates topography extended into the library and split-level organization.[10, 11] The newest location for the library will comprise of six levels, fully accessible via barrier-free sloping walkways.[12]

THE HITCHHIKING GHOST

The University of British Columbia Library
Vancouver, British Columbia

There is certainly no shortage of urban legends about ghostly hitchhikers. But one particular hitchhiker appears only to young male drivers on dark and broody nights: a lone and oddly silent female with an unearthly desire to get to the UBC library.

The legend tells of an accident that took place in the 1960s. Apparently, while driving one rainy evening along University Avenue en route to the UBC campus library, a young couple got into a heated argument. Frustrated, the woman demanded that the man stop the car, after which she got out, determined to walk the rest of the way to the library by herself. The woman never made it to the library, as she was struck by another car and died instantly.[13, 14]

Since that stormy night, numerous male students have shared a similar story: while driving on bleary, overcast, and rainy evenings, they have pulled over to pick up a lone female hitchhiker standing in the rain. In each case, the woman said nothing, merely handed the driver a piece of paper with the library's address on it, and then hopped into the back seat, only to disappear almost immediately.[15]

It seems that this poor woman, no matter how many attempts she makes, is destined never to arrive at her desired destination. It is too bad, because if she did reach the library, there might be a ghostly companion with which she could commune. Paranormal Studies and Investigations Canada (PSICAN) not only publishes reports about the legend of the female hitchhiker, but also tales of an old woman in a white dress. She allegedly appears inside the university library, but vanishes into thin air if approached.[16, 17]

The UBC Library website shares these as well as other creepy stories. In an October 2013 article about the unusual and the haunted, Andrea Coutts wrote about odd phenomena in the Irving K. Barbara Learning Centre — staff reports that books spontaneously jumped off shelves. Perhaps more chillingly, Managing Librarian Julie Mitchell reported hearing the sound of typing coming from Room 203 multiple times, but each time she checked the room, she found it empty.[18]

HAUNTED COUNTRY BOOKSHOP

The Country Bookshop

Lloydtown, Ontario

When the Country Bookshop in Lloydtown closed down there were over 15,000 books on its shelves — and one legend of a mysterious hooded lady.[19]

The ghost never walked through the bookshop, but immediately outside it. "She is a solid-looking figure," owner Art Gray said. "A lady in a cloak, hooded. You never see her face."[20]

Gray explained that at twilight, the woman would start walking from the walnut tree at the top of the driveway and slowly move up and down the driveway, as if searching for something.[21]

There is a local legend from the early 1900s that takes place on the land The Country Bookshop was located on, in which a young mother suffered the tragic loss of her baby. It is unclear whether the baby died or was taken from the woman, but the ending is the same: a ghostly apparition continually and endlessly searches for the lost child every single night after sundown.[22]

"Many people have seen her," Gray explains. "But she doesn't bother anyone. She's quite harmless, part of the family really." Apparently dogs wag their tales in the presence of the apparition.[23]

The bookstore might no longer exist, but the hooded woman likely continues on her endless quest, forever searching for her lost baby long into the night.

> The Country Bookshop was originally opened in 1967 by bibliophile Art Gray. Gray, a life-long book lover, was particularly fond of books about Canadian history and pioneer life. He ran the bookstore from the day he opened it in 1967 until his death in 1984. Gray's widow, Audrey, ran the store for a few years following her husband's death, before finally closing its doors for good.[24]

THE RUNNYMEDE GHOST

Chapters Runnymede
Toronto, Ontario

In some locations, businesses come and go, but ghosts abide. Such is the case in an old theatrical locale that was most recently known and beloved as a neighbourhood bookstore. But it's the building's history that gives it its ghostly inhabitants, including a little girl who can sometimes be heard eerily crying from the old stage.

The Runnymede Theatre, located in Bloor West Village in the west end of Toronto, was built in 1927 to be an atmospheric vaudeville style theatre, with such features as white clouds painted on the ceiling and tiny lights meant to simulate stars in the night sky. It was Canada's first theatre of its kind. In the late 1930s it was converted into a movie theatre, and was declared an historic building in 1990.[25] After much controversy in the neighbourhood, big box store Chapters moved into the location, spending over $3.5 million in restoration efforts.

Legends shared about the old Runnymede Theatre include that of a little girl who apparently died right on the theatre's stage in the early 1900s. The various local legends are unclear about who the girl was, whether she was performing as an actor or was the child of one of the performers, but they do all say the little girl died when a sandbag dropped onto her from the ceiling.

While there do not seem to be any official records of such a death taking place in the theatre, there have been repeated reports from people who claim to have heard the sound of a child crying and witnessed the ghostly spectre of a little girl. These accounts come from the time Runnymede was a theatre through to the fifteen years that it was a popular bookstore haunt.

A former Runnymede theatre manager reported being in the basement supply area, located beneath the stage, and becoming suddenly overwhelmed with a woozy feeling before seeing the figure of a little girl standing before him for a few seconds, after which she completely disappeared.[26]

Chapters Runnymede.

One woman remembers a performance she and her husband attended for singer Mike Ford at the Chapters: "During the performance I heard a child crying," she writes. "I looked around to see where the child was, but then realized that the child was actually magnified coming out of the speakers." It was only after she returned home and looked into the history of the building that she learned about the little girl who allegedly died on the stage.[27]

Former Runnymede Chapters staff have also reported odd occurrences while working there, including the overwhelming sensation of being watched, cold chills, and dizziness when standing on the stage area; books flying off shelves all on their own; unexplainable glimpses of figures disappearing down bookstore aisles out of the corner of their eye; and the appearance of sand on the stage area floor with no easy explanation as to where it could have come from.[28, 29]

Chapters Runnymede closed down in February 2014, and a Shopper's Drug Mart is slated to take over the location. One can't help but wonder if the ghost that roamed both the theatre and the bookstore will continue to appear to the new staff and customers.

In the late 1930s the Runnymede Theatre stopped being used for plays and live entertainment and was converted into a movie theatre. As an historic building, there was significant controversy when, after a search that lasted nineteen months, Chapters stepped up as a company that was willing to preserve the theatre's original unique theatrical façade. Almost two thousand local residents signed a petition protesting the move and what was seen as the "threat" of the big box store's arrival into this culturally significant landmark.[30]

Even the final film screened in the theatre seemed to be sending a message about what was happening. *You've Got Mail*, a romantic comedy starring Tom Hanks and Meg Ryan about a big box bookstore chain forcing a quaint local mom-and-pop independent bookstore out of business, played in the theatre on February 28, 1999.[31]

However, when the big-box chain giant spent over $3.5 million to restore and renovate the theatre back to its former glory, even the skeptics and most adamant protesters seemed to appreciate how the space could continue to maintain a unique element of history and culture, as it became recognized as one of the most beautiful bookstore spaces in the world.[32, 33]

In 2013, with the same sense of loss area residents felt when their beloved theatre was closing, the neighbourhood rallied together to take up a petition to try to save the bookstore that, facing rent increases that exceeded its operating budget, had no choice but to close.[34]

But the decision had already been made; despite the support, the financials were just not feasible. Chapters Runnymede closed its doors on February 16, 2014, staying open until 9:00 p.m. and playing music from the 20s and 30s as an homage to the beautiful theatre.

Shoppers Drug Mart, which opened in that location in the summer of 2014, promised to retain all of the existing historical features, including the stage and unique inside walls.[35]

GHOSTS IN THE ATTIC

Attic Books
London, Ontario

Attic Books in London, Ontario, is home to a pair of eerie beings. A gargoyle keeps watch outside, while inside, the resident ghost takes care of the haunting. Bookstore staff claim that, ever since the move to its current location, the bookstore has been home to a ghost with a penchant for cigars and who is, in fact, a bit of a bookworm.[36]

Cassandra MacVicar, one of the store's managers, says that the staff started calling the ghost Roland.[37] Roland makes himself known by the strong odour of cigar smoke (despite there being no trace of actual smoke anywhere in the building) that wafts up the stairs from the basement to the main floor. Basement lights flicker on and off, and books fall off the shelf for no apparent reason.[38]

The staff provided Roland with a wooden chair from the 1930s and place books on the chair as a way to keep the spirit occupied. The chair sits in a back corner of the basement storage room and acts like a talisman: it seems that providing the spirit with books keeps its activities to a minimum.[39]

A local research group called Paranormal Knights of London Investigators visited Attic Books and drafted a report on their findings. They detected a man wearing a wristband with a pin cushion on top and with a name that begins with an A.[40] Historians note that the very first resident of the building, who moved in in 1875, was a tailor by the name of Abraham Spry. The description given by the Paranormal Knights seems to suggest that Roland is in fact the ghost of Abraham Spry, but the Knights encountered the presence on the third floor, a location that did not exist when Spry was a resident of the building.[41] Furthermore, the staff detected Roland in the basement, not the third floor.

The possibility that the ghost is that of George Reid, one of the brothers who occupied the building from 1881 to 1886, has also been explored. But Reid was a vehement non-drinker and non-smoker, so the cigar smoke wafting from the basement doesn't make sense.[42]

With a large and rather diverse stock of antique books, maps, and prints, as well as discount books, Attic Books continues to appeal to a wide range of customers. This includes, perhaps, one unidentified long-time resident who enjoys the luxury of phantom cigars and being surrounded by books.

One of Canada's largest independent used and antiquarian bookstores, Attic Books in London, Ontario, has been in business since 1976. The store, which fulfilled a personal dream of owner Marvin Post, originally opened on the top floor of a building on Richmond Street, and then moved to an upper floor on Clarence Street. Both of these locations leant beautifully to the store's name. Downtown development of the Galleria Mall in 1987 forced the shop to move right out of town, to Parkhill, Ontario, but Post worked with London mayor Diane Haskett to bring the shop back to its hometown to its current location at 240 Dundas Street.[43, 44]

Attic Books is now situated in a Late Victorian Red Brick Commercial building that originally was a single storey and only about twenty feet long. Renovations in 1880 and 1919 brought a second and third storey to the building, as well as significantly increased space, accommodating a mezzanine. Large pane glass windows were installed in the 1930s. That, and the gargoyle added in 1996, give the store an historic and eerie feel from the outside.

SPIRITS OF THE POORHOUSE WRETCHED

The Spring Garden Road Memorial Public Library

Halifax, Nova Scotia

Some employees at the Spring Garden Road Memorial Library are leery about working late, particularly in the basement. After sundown, inexplicable dark human shapes appear, moving about in the shadows, and eerie breathing can sometimes be heard. Some believe the phenomenon comes from the ghost of a long-forgotten library clerk, while others think it might have something to do with the building's location and its history.[45]

Built in 1951 as a monument commemorating Halifax's casualties from the two World Wars, the library was built upon a graveyard, but not an official graveyard; the official one, St. Paul's Cemetery, sits directly across the street. The graveyard here was a makeshift one known as the Poor House Cemetery.[46]

In Halifax in the 1750s there were those who could afford houses, and those who couldn't (mostly widows, orphans, wounded soldiers, the sick, and the mentally ill) lived in a large wooden building constructed by the Governor's Council and nicknamed "The Poor House."[47]

Looking much like a creepy old haunted house from a classic horror movie, The Poor House sported a whipping post and stocks on the front lawn. Several times a week, a large man named Hawkins would tie inmates of the house to the post and attempt to whip the devil out of them.[48]

Life expectancy of residents of The Poor House was relatively short, and the dead were not welcome in St. Paul's Cemetery. Instead, their bodies were buried in shallow graves in various locations about the grounds. Local prisoners and those who were hanged were also buried there, as were the lower ranks of a regiment of American Revolution soldiers returning from battle who were stricken with a deadly fever.[49]

By 1814, The Poor House was converted into a type of correctional facility for short-term confinement and punishment for petty offenders known as a bridewell. The keeper of the bridewell was known to exact harsh cruelty on the inmates. Public floggings and residents wearing spiked collars while chained to a fence outdoors were not uncommon. Shallow graves with exposed appendages of the dead sticking out of the ground in some spots were also a regular occurrence.[50]

While most of the bodies were exhumed before Grafton Park and the library were established, the spirits of the dead are said to remain. One doesn't need to imagine the decades of tortured souls howling their cries deep into the night. Some ghostly sounds are still heard, including reports of library staff hearing eerie and disembodied breathing when there is nobody around. Others have reported seeing an odd male figure prowling in the shadows among the stacks, wearing what has been described as "old-fashioned" clothing; he isn't seen for long because he has a habit of vanishing into thin air when anybody approaches him.[51, 52]

These sounds and the odd, eerie disappearing man might be the result of folklore and vivid imaginations, or they just might be previous tenants whose spirits are forever trapped roaming the grounds were they lived, were tortured, and were eventually buried.

Located in the heart of the city of Halifax (5381 Spring Garden Road), The Spring Garden Road Memorial Public Library opened in 1951 on the site of Grafton Park as a memorial to Halifax's casualties in the First and Second World Wars. With over 228,000 titles and housing an extension reference collection, this library branch is the largest in the region.[53]

Opening its doors on November 12, 1951, the library was warmly received by patrons. In its first week over 1,300 patrons came through the library, signing out more than two thousand books. By the end of the first year, over 200,000 items had been loaned out.[54]

THE ROCKING CHAIR GHOST

Thornhill Village Library
Thornhill, Ontario

There was something a little odd in the specification sheet handed out by Thornhill Village Library staff in 2010:

Building Features

- 4,283 sq. ft.
- 7 public use computers
- Seating for 20
- One of few remaining buildings in the Classical Revival style in the GTA with no alterations to front façade.
- Surrounded by Thornhill Village Heritage Garden — maintained in a late-Victorian style.

- Drawings by Thoreau MacDonald, plus various historic documents and photographs relating to the village of Thornhill on display.
- Resident ghost

Yes, you read that correctly: "Resident ghost."

Before it was renovated into the Thornhill Village Library in 1959, the clapboard house, built in 1851, was a private home. Since then, the building has also functioned as a grocery store and as a veterinary office; at one time there was even a stable around back, well before additions and renovations to the building increased its size and shape. The Ontario Heritage Act designated the building as a unique example of a modern domestic building of the Classical Revival Style.[55]

Thornhill Public Library.

And, although it is now a public building, the library appears to be home to at least one resident ghost, if not two.

One of the first encounters with a ghostly resident in the building took place on a quiet afternoon in March 1972. A male library patron by the name of Gene Gerry was browsing in a back room of the library when his nostrils were assailed by a terribly strong skunk odour. Immediately following this, he noticed a kindly old woman sitting in an antique rocking chair, perfectly situated in a ray of sunshine from a nearby window. As he watched her, he could hear her quietly muttering "John, John, John." Gerry turned to get his wife's attention in order to point out the woman, but when he turned back, the woman had vanished.

Gerry was adamant that he saw an old lady in the rocking chair, but his wife would not believe him. He was so upset that he wrote a letter to the Woodbridge and Vaughn News asking for any other witnesses who might also have seen the strange vision to come forth. "If you could find out if anyone has ever seen this lady, even one person, well, just let my wife know, then I will be vindicated," he wrote.[56]

The same old lady was seen by a page one afternoon. A staff member recalls pausing while shelving books to look over at the page, who was standing at the bottom of the stairs, frozen in place, with her face pale. When she approached the page to ask what the matter was, the youth did not initially want to say. Eventually, she relayed the fact that she had seen the ghost of an old woman standing at the top of the stairs; the bottom of a dress, crinoline, and old fashioned granny boots stuck out in her mind.

Another page reported that she was organizing books on the children's cart when she noticed a woman in white rushing past her in a hurry. The page watched after the woman, only to see that the farther the woman in white moved away from her, the more transparent she became, until she seemed to disappeared into thin air.

A regular patron of the library reported to staff that he had witnessed what appeared to be an old woman looking down at him from one of the upstairs windows when he was walking past the building one evening, long after the library had closed.

Other staff members have also provided evidence of what they believe to be the same old lady, but without actually seeing the ghost. Sometimes they hear the squeaky sounds of springs, as if someone were sitting in the empty rocking chair. Other times they hear the sounds of an old woman coughing and fidgeting, almost convincing themselves that someone was sitting in the chair, impatiently waiting for someone by the window.[57]

Staff also got used to the daily routine that the ghost seemed to have. Every evening they would overhear noises coming from upstairs, the same footfall pattern as though someone were walking around, preparing for bed.[58]

Former librarian Betsey Boyden says that after perhaps a dozen instances when she went upstairs to check on the footfall, she finally gave up because there was never anybody up there. She doesn't have an answer as to what it might be, but she did say she sometimes caught the scent of something unusual, like brimstone, in the air.[59]

Boyden also recalled the reaction a German schnauzer had after it fixated on some unseen object in the front room of the library. "It was riveted with fright and growled," Boyden said as she described how the dog pulled on its leash and seemed to keep its eyes fixed on something that was moving across the empty room.[60] "All of a sudden, he bristled up and he growled. His head turned and he watched something all the way around the room."[61]

"You were always aware of something there," Boyden said. "I don't know what it was, but you always had a feeling you weren't alone."[62]

Another staff member recalled an odd incident that happened when she was working one evening. She had been standing near the front window, cleaning the coffee pot in the front parlour, when all of a sudden she heard two sets of feet running and jumping directly upstairs in the local history room. The footsteps were light, as if made by children. There were no patrons around at the time, just her and another staff member.

She thought it was odd that they could even hear footfall to begin with: "We had recently put new carpet down, so one shouldn't be able to hear footsteps," she says. "To this day, I have never been able to hear the clear and solid sound of feet upstairs due to the muffling of the carpet."

She then heard shutters slamming open and closed. It was another odd thing, since she knew that the shutters were bolted open. When she turned and looked out to the street, she saw the front gate swing open and closed, all by itself.

It was an odd series of events to hear and witness, but she says she felt calm while the whole thing was happening. When she explained the situation the next day to the branch head, she was told that other people had remarked at just how calm and comfortable they felt after being "allowed" to see the resident ghost.

Cynthia Tappay, branch librarian, worked in the building for more than fifteen years and shared several occurrences experienced by herself and others. Like her colleague, she claims to have had a feeling of warmth and peace in the building, "from all the people who have used the library, as well as from those who have lived in the building over the years since 1851."[63]

Tappay recounted a time she had been standing in the parlour with two contractors who were installing new track lighting. One of the men commented that he could smell a strong burning smell, but neither Tappay nor the other contractor smelled anything.[64]

Both Tappay and Boyden shared stories of other unexplained phenomenon that have occurred in the building, such as a clock that ran backwards, the front door opening and closing on its own, and the distinct sounds of books being placed firmly on shelves, or furniture being moved in an adjacent vacant room.[65, 66]

"I haven't even decided if I believe in ghosts," Tappay said. "If it is a ghost, I don't think it's unfriendly. I'm not nervous of it."[67]

She went on to add. "If a house is old, you sometimes think that people leave an impression on the house, sort of an echo from the past. Who knows?"[68]

"Having said this," Tappay said, "I will also add that I do not intend to spend Halloween night or any other night in the building, for at night the library belongs to previous occupants."[69]

Finally, she added: "I myself may someday haunt the building."[70]

HAUNTED HISTORY BOOKS

Rivendell Books

Barrie, Ontario

Imagine walking into a used bookstore and bringing back not just a great book to read, but also an unseen spirit trapped within its pages. Talk about a supernatural "buy one item, get another item for free" experience.

That is exactly what happened to a man who purchased a book about the First World War from Rivendell Books, a used bookstore in Barrie.[71] Derek Ellis's first thought when he woke at 12:04 a.m. and spied a man standing at the foot of his bed, was that he was still sleeping. But he was awake and looking at a very solid image of a man wearing a brown coat that went down to his ankles, with a rope tied around his waist.[72]

This was the first of several appearances that the strange apparition made in the Ellis home.

Another night, Ellis woke to the sound of someone flipping through the pages of a book. When he opened his eyes, he saw the same man he had seen before standing in front of the closet door. "The figure had the book in his hands," Ellis said in an interview with the *Barrie Examiner*. The figure was turned away from him, so at first Ellis thought it might be his wife, "But then," he said, "it put the book down on the dresser and walked away from me, closer toward the closet, and before he went through the door he waved at me."[73] Ellis was startled to see the man disappear through the door into his closet because the man had appeared to be entirely solid.[74]

With each appearance, different strange events occurred. One night Ellis heard the chair at the side of his bed creaking, as if someone were getting up from it or sitting down. Another night, he smelled the powerful scent of a bouquet of flowers, even though there was no floral arrangement in the room. Once he woke to see the closet door replaced by a red curtain, tied in the middle with a red ribbon, an image that slowly dissolved back to the solid closet door.[75]

"Even now I look in the closet before going to bed," Ellis said. He even had the overwhelming urge to check the closet when he woke in the middle of the night to go to the bathroom. "It's disturbing," he added.[76]

Frustrated and confused, Ellis went to speak to a local priest. The priest suggested that the spirit haunting Ellis's home was somehow attached to the book he had purchased, and recommended that he return the book to the store.[77]

When Ellis explained to Wendy Cahill, the store's owner, about why he was returning the book, Cahill believed him immediately.[78] Cahill and her customers had reported multiple unexplainable occurrences in her Wellington Street store, most of which were attributed to the ghost of an elderly man.[79]

"He's here because he likes the books," Cahill said in an interview with the *Barrie Examiner*, stating that everyone who had seen him tended to describe him in similar terms: an elderly, grey-haired man with old fashioned clothing. "I've had customers come up to me and say he appeared in front of them and actually touched them."[80]

Cahill recounted the time a woman was smoking a cigarette outside while waiting for a prescription to be filled at a nearby pharmacy when she spotted the elderly man walking back and forth in front of the store. "Then," Cahill said, "he walked right through the glass."[81]

Cahill recounted times when she and her husband would return to the store the morning after a late Saturday evening of tidying and counting inventory, only to discover stacks of books piled in the centre of the floor.[82]

"By the time we leave [at night] we know everything is in order, and there's nothing on the floor when we leave," Cahill said. "But when we came back Sunday mornings we were finding books neatly stacked in piles on the floor."[83]

"The books found in piles tended to always be in one specific area of the store," Cahill explained. "They're always in this one particular area of our military section, where we have books about World War I and World War II."[84]

A book about Charles Manson also brought shivers to Cahill's spine. One evening she heard a big thump near the front of the store. When she investigated the noise she found the Charles Manson book, which had been located on a shelf at the back of the store, lying on the floor, with Manson's face on the front grinning up at her. "It really creeped me out," she said.[85]

Erin Gauthier, Angela Snowden, and Deborah Johnson, known as the *Ghost Girls of Simcoe County* (on Rogers TV), investigated the haunted bookshop for one of their first episodes.

Gauthier recounted that the bookstore was the scariest place they have investigated, stating that there was more than one spirit present at the location. "There's something in that back room," Gauthier said. "I wanted to do our investigation in the back room and books were falling, and our energy gauge went crazy. It was a weird, awkward feeling like someone was watching us over our shoulders the whole time."

So far, no other customers have reported any of Rivendell Books' ghosts following them home the way they followed Derek Ellis. However, it certainly makes you wonder if the next used book you purchase may not only be filled with information, knowledge and wonder, but also the spirit of its former reader.

INUIT CARVING DISPLAY MYSTERY
Terryberry Branch, Hamilton Public Library
Hamilton, Ontario

In legends, spiritual forces tend to be stronger and more con-
centrated at crossroads. Such might be the case for a particular Hamilton library branch that rests on a well-established
crossroads for travellers, where I experienced a personal meeting with a spirit.

The Terryberry branch of the Hamilton Public Library was
built on land once owned by William Terryberry and his wife, Anne
Young. Terryberry and his wife constructed a two-and-a-half-sto-
rey inn on a route which, prior to the War of 1812, was a popular stage coach stopover for travellers journeying from Niagara to
Ancaster. Built in 1810 and demolished in 1897, the first official
public meeting in Upper Canada was held at the inn in 1816.

And just as the historic Terryberry Inn served as a local
community meeting place, used for dances and other special

occasions and public gatherings, so too does this library branch today.

The Terryberry branch has been my local library since I moved to the city in 1997. Prior to the most recent renovation, my son and I spent Saturday mornings there, selecting our weekly reading material and playing in the popular children's learn-and-play area on the main level.

When I did an October 2013 talk about my book *Haunted Hamilton: The Ghosts of Dundurn Castle & Other Steeltown Shivers* in the basement hall at the Terryberry branch, two eerie incidents were brought to my attention, which made me reflect on the power of such a locale.

The first happened the evening I gave my talk and reading. After it was over and I was hanging around to speak with folks and sign copies of my books, a woman who had been sitting in the first row approached me and introduced herself as a medium.

"There was someone standing behind you the whole time you were speaking," she told me. "Just over your right shoulder."

I shuddered at the thought and felt goosebumps rise on my arms and the hair stand up on the back of my neck.

Though I write about ghostly occurrences, I'm one of the biggest chickens you'll ever meet. I was thankful not to have felt anything odd while doing the talk — I was creeped out enough just sharing a few spooky tales.

She went on to say that "he" was no longer present, and that the presence was a positive one. That made me feel a bit better, although I was still a little nervous about the whole thing. I asked her to describe what she'd seen, or who she thought it might be. She said she didn't know, but described him as a man who was middle-aged or perhaps older and that he was simply observing me, perhaps in a supportive manner.

I immediately took comfort in what she said, believing that she might have seen my father, who died more than ten years ago, standing at my back, watching over me, perhaps even looking on at me with pride and fatherly love.

So, while I had interpreted what she described as something of personal significance to me, I later heard a story from library staff that makes me think the spirit could have been someone else: prior to the most recent renovation, the second floor of the library housed a small display case of Inuit carvings. When nobody was watching, the soapstone figures would mysteriously move on their own.

The figures' origins, as provided by Terryberry library staff, might begin to explain the strange phenomenon:

> The Mountain Sanatorium opened in 1906 and became the largest centre for the treatment of tuberculosis in the British Commonwealth. Unfortunately, when the disease had almost been conquered it took hold in the Native population in the Arctic. Between 1954 and 1963, over a thousand Inuit patients passed through the doors of the old San. Since treatment for tuberculosis took twelve to eighteen months, many become homesick. Many of the patients carved figures to pass the time and some of them went on to gain international recognition. The figures in this case were donated by J. Kulpa. The bear and the Inuit man were carved by Oowalayoo. The char was done by Noah Aglat and the loon probably by Moses Mecko. Noah Aragutana carved the walrus and the goose was done by Peter Saunders.

Is it possible that the figures themselves contain residue of the homesick patients who carved them? Could the carvings be shuffled about by the spirits of travellers who frequently stayed on those very lands when it was the popular Terryberry Inn? Or could it merely be vibrations from buses and other traffic on nearby Mohawk Road? Perhaps, as community librarian Sophie Gorsky speculates, it might be subtle breezes and disturbances from nearby doors opening and closing.

Whatever it is, speculation about the mystery of the moving Inuit carvings at Terryberry are very much a reminder of the crossroads that has been a popular gathering place for over two hundred years.

Prior to the most recent renovation in February of 2012, which included an increased display and marketplace area, barrier-free washrooms, and a larger children's area, the Terryberry Branch underwent a renovation in 1990 and 1991 to include a second floor that provided additional collection space along with an expanded and improved reading and studying space.

GO TOWARD THE LIGHT!

Coles Bookstore

North Bay, Ontario

The presence of ghosts often spooks people, but sometimes, they can be just downright annoying.

That's the case in a story involving bookseller Rob Evans. Evans, currently the manager for Coles in the New Sudbury Shopping Centre, has always been an enthusiastic supporter of authors, eagerly welcoming them into his store, where they are made to feel at home. He isn't that way with every visitor to the store, though — at least not the preternatural visitors — evidenced through this story he shared with me when I was at his store signing copies of my book, *Spooky Sudbury*.

The Coles store in North Bay, where Evans used to work, "used to be a strip mall with a row of stores on the lower level, including the Coles," he said, "and upstairs were some apartments." It was in those upstairs apartments where, allegedly, a woman had died.

Over the years, people claimed to have seen and heard strange things in the store. The staff were perplexed by repeated occurrences of dozens of books being knocked off shelves and found in piles when they returned to the store in the mornings. Sometimes, they found piled books in the middle of the day in a section that had been vacant.

"Books fall off the shelves all the time," Evans said. "Typically in particularly humid seasons when the paper absorbs moisture in the air and changes weight and shape. And it's usually only the front book in a faced-out display, particularly when it's already close to the edge of the shelf." But these instances were a bit more haphazard, and looked as though an unseen hand had swept the books off the shelves.

While Rob had never seen or heard any other strange things in the years he worked at the store, he heard reports from staff and customers who claimed to have seen something that looked like a person out of the corner of their eye. When they turned to look, however, nobody was there. One of the descriptions of this mysterious figure identified it as a middle-aged woman dressed in clothing that looked like it was from the 1950s or 1960s.

Rob never really believed the stories, or that the store was haunted. The tales shared with him were certainly fun, though, and an intriguing way to explain the books repeatedly knocked from the shelves. But sometimes, when you are tired and feeling desperate, you clutch at virtually any kind of answer to an ongoing issue.

Frustrated one day with what felt like the thousandth time he had to reshelve a pile of "downed" books, Rob yelled to the ghost: "Go toward the light!"

He can't be sure if it helped, since shortly after the incident he was promoted to a position at a different location. He knows it certainly felt good to try to do something about the constant annoyance. If a lost spirit was indeed stranded on the earthly plane, maybe all it needed was for someone to say it was okay to move on to the next world.

At his current location in Sudbury, neither Rob nor any of his staff have encountered anything other than the occasional book falling to the floor, as sometimes happens — and they are just fine with that.

THE SHADOWY FIGURE

Art Gallery of Ontario

Toronto, Ontario

A shadowy figure often moves through the library of the Grange, just one of several ghostly inhabitants of the historic building on Dundas Street West in Toronto. Originally built in 1817 as the private home of D'Arcy Boulton Jr., the Grange was located on one hundred acres of land. Over the years, changes in ownership and land sales eventually found the building housing the Art Gallery of Toronto. In 1966, it was renamed the Art Gallery of Ontario.

In 1995, Connie Masters wrote the following in the April issue of *The Grange Newsletter*:

> Are we sharing the house with others (apart from the resident ants, mice, and moths)? With any house of the age of the Grange, supernatural manifestations are not unusual. Does something

forever remain of intense emotion experienced by those who have lived happily or unhappily within the walls? Many Grangers have heard the story (and some knew her) of the cleaner who was working alone in the house one day when it was closed to the public. As she was about to go up the staircase to the second floor she looked up, only to see the figure of a man standing at the top staring down at her. Needless to say, she dropped her utensils, and beat a hasty retreat back to the gallery, vowing never to work in the Grange again . . . and she didn't.[86]

In his book *Haunted Toronto*, John Robert Colombo shares a lengthy letter from Elayne Dobel Goyette, who was a guide in the Grange between 1989 and 1993. Goyette sensed three distinct presences in the home. She encountered a ghost that she described as "the Gentleman in the yellow coat," who materialized right out of a wall, brush against her arm as he walked past her, through the drawing room, and exited through another wall which, at one time, had been a corridor. She also encountered what she calls "the Lady in Black" in what was the young girl's bedroom on the second floor, as well as "the Lady in White," whose frightening presence Goyette felt near the main-floor stairwell that leads to the basement kitchen.[87]

Some believe that Goldwyn Smith (1823-1910), one of the last residents of the property before it became a museum, is the shadowy male figure seen moving about the library.[88] Others believe that the ghost might be that of William Chin, the man who was butler at the Grange for fifty years. Chin, who kept a household ledger, made his final entry on September 30, 1910 with a note that read: "Left dear old Grange at 1:00 o'clock p.m. to be wanderer."[89]

There is further speculation that the library might be haunted by Algernon Blackwood, who worked in the study assisting Goldwyn Smith in his literary endeavours between 1890 and 1892. Interestingly, Blackwood later went on to become one of the most prolific writers of ghost stories in the history of the genre, with more than a dozen novels, a half-dozen plays, and over 140 short, "weird fiction" tales to his name. H.P. Lovecraft named Algernon one of the four modern masters of horror, alongside Arthur Machen, Lord Dunsany, and M.R. James.[90, 91, 92] Could he be spending his afterlife spooking people as he did in life?

Originally built in 1817 as the home of D'Arcy Boulton Jr. and his family, the Grange was located on land that extended from Queen Street in the south to Bloor Street in the north and from Beverly Street in the east to McCaul Street in the west. The original building was two storeys high, approximately sixty by forty feet in area, and reflected a sense of Georgian balance, with the front door opening onto a central hall, with a dining room on the left and a drawing room on the right.[93]

The north section of the property was sold to Bishop Strachan in 1828 in order to be used for King's College, and property to the south was donated in the 1840s for the establishment of St. George the Martyr Church and St. Patrick's Market.[94]

By the turn of the century it was decided that Toronto should have an art gallery. The building had, by then, transferred ownership via marriage and the property was left to become The Art Museum of Toronto in 1910. By 1966 it was renamed the Art Gallery of Ontario and has today become a vibrant part of bringing people together.[95, 96]

SPECTRES IN THE STACKS

McLennan Library, McGill University

Montreal, Quebec

The Rare Books and Special Collections department of the McLennan Library at McGill University began collecting rare materials in the 1850s and contains dozens of unique special collections.[97]

Beyond the physical holdings, however, its special collections are known to contain "more things in heaven and earth" than might be dreamt of in more typical university philosophies. There might indeed be a spectre in the stacks of this building, perhaps brought there via a bloody cloth that is on display in the collection.

The spectre appears to be an old man in what is described as old-fashioned attire, and is said to haunt the sixth floor of the library. When the ghost is addressed, he reportedly looks directly at the person speaking before disappearing.[98]

One explanation for the ghost sits on the fourth floor of the library, behind a locked door and encased in glass: a piece of cloth stained with the brown, mottled blood of Abraham Lincoln. The towel was applied to the president's head shortly after he was shot by John Wilkes Booth.[99]

Booth himself made brief visits to Montreal prior to his assassination of Lincoln. His plan, after murdering the president, had been to flee to Canada to seek political refuge. Booth never made it to Canada, as he was shot down in a barn in Virginia, but one of the items found on his person included a bank receipt from the Royal Ontario Bank in Montreal.[100]

Perhaps Wilkes's spirit returned to Montreal and wanders about *The Joseph N. Nathanson Collection of Lincolniana*, an eclectic collection, which includes Dr. Nathanson's extensive collection of over four thousand monographs, prints, images, portraits, badges, and other memorabilia collected over the course of fifty years.[101]

Of course, the McLennan Library isn't the only haunted location on the McGill campus. The founder of the university, James McGill, had his remains reinterred near the front of the Arts building in 1875, and his ghost is often seen guarding the university wearing a tricorne hat made of beaver fur. The ashes of William Osler, one of the most renowned members of the McGill Faculty of Medicine, rest in a niche at the Osler Library. Osler, who died in 1919 at the age of seventy, bestowed a significant portion of his rare collection of books and manuscripts to the library. Legend has it that students studying late into the night at this particular library might just catch a glimpse of the ghost of Osler leafing through one of his many beloved old manuscripts.[102]

Staff of the McLennan Library building pride themselves on the range and quality of the collections and services they provide to the McGill community, and they seek to ensure an active learning and research space for all.[103]

The building, named after Isabella McLennan, who donated a fortune for the purchase of books, was constructed on the northeast corner of Sherbrooke and McTavish between 1967 and 1969, and stands on the site of what was once a mansion owned by Jessie Joseph.[104]

The Rare Books and Special Collections department of the library contains dozens of unique special collections, including the extensive *History of the Book* collection.[105]

THE MIRACULOUS SURVIVAL OF THE PARLIAMENTARY LIBRARY

The Library of Parliament
Ottawa, Ontario

While there are no alleged ghosts walking the Parliamentary Library in Ottawa, there just might be something beyond this world that has allowed it to survive despite terrible odds.

The fact that the library stands today, despite multiple disasters that threatened to destroy it, is a testament not only to the foresight of librarian Alpheus Todd and a library clerk, but perhaps also to some unseen presence that continues to guard the building.

Todd insisted both on the "chapter house" style design of the building, which kept the library separated from the main parliamentary buildings, as well as the iron fire doors that were part of the design.[106] So when the fire alarm sounded on February 3, 1916, at 8:37 p.m., quick-thinking library clerk Connolly "Connie" McCormac ensured that the iron fire doors were slammed shut before evacuating the building.[107, 108]

The iron fire doors helped prevent the fire, which completely destroyed the main parliament buildings, from reaching the library. The fire had allegedly spread from a smouldering cigar in a wastebasket, through the recently oiled wooden interior walls and the just-varnished floors. There was also a high wind coming in from the northwest that caught the growing fire just west of the library and swept it toward the senate.[109] Around midnight, the bell in the Victoria Tower crashed to the ground, with eyewitnesses claiming that it was overtaken by flames only after completing the midnight chime. The fire department worked through the night, valiantly trying to bring the disastrous blaze under control.[110, 111]

That fateful night in 1916 wasn't the first time the library was threatened and it certainly wouldn't be the last.

Early in the Library of Parliament's history, the Legislature and its library moved from Kingston to Montreal and then alternated between Toronto and Quebec City for several years, before finding a permanent home in Ottawa in 1857. The most disastrous blaze that threatened the library during that time was when a Loyalist mob protesting the Rebellion Losses Bill burned down the Legislature and destroyed all but two hundred of its twelve thousand books.[112]

In 1952, an electrical short in the roof of the library caused a fire that almost destroyed the entire building. Firefighters cut through the metal roof in order to put out the flames that were spreading beneath the library's dome, causing flood and water damage. But for the second time, the library itself survived any major disaster.

Was it blind luck or an otherworldly presence that has continued to protect the library from one of books' most devastating enemies? Could it be fearless librarian Alpheus Todd, continuing on his mission of keeping his beloved library safe? Or perhaps a former politician, trapped forever in parliament, keeping an eye on the Canadian treasures that the library holds?

There is more than seventeen kilometres of materials in the Main Library Building's collection and over half a million items covering hundreds of years of Canada's history, including government documents, periodicals, books, and videos, along with a plethora of digital resources such as electronic news filtering systems and online databases. It accommodates a reading room for parliamentarians, a reference desk, a rare book room, offices, and an expanded area for visitors.[113, 114]

Considered a Gothic Revival Marvel, the building, separated from the main body of Centre Block by a corridor, is the central hub of a larger complex that spreads to other parliamentary buildings. Designed by Thomas Fuller and Chilion Jones, with input from librarian Alpheus Todd, the load-bearing walls are supported by a ring of sixteen flying buttresses, double-wythe masonry made up of a hydraulic lime rubble fill core and finished stone and rustic Nepean sandstone. Stone trim adorns the windows and edges, featuring stone carvings, floral patterns, and friezes meant to match the Victorian High Gothic style of the rest of the parliamentary buildings. The roof, which is set in three tiers topped by a cupola, is covered in a deck made out of copper.[115]

GOOSEBUMPS AT SMITHBOOKS

Smithbooks, Sherway Gardens

Etobicoke, Ontario

The ghostly residents of many beloved bookstore locations that are now closed continue to haunt the hearts and minds of both patrons and staff members. These spirits are all the more memorable if, like any good customer, they display a penchant for a particular author's books.

I was intrigued to chat with an old bookseller colleague about an experience that she had when she worked at a bookstore that has been closed now for about fourteen years. Even though Shannon left the store back in 1998, she kept with her a fond and deep love for the bookstore, her fellow staff members, and the customers of the Smithbooks at Sherway Gardens.

Shannon described the kids' section as being separated from the rest of the store with a little arch, and that on one side of the aisle there was a growing collection of R.L. Stine's Goosebumps books, with a similar collection of Christopher Pike novels on the other side. Both series fell into huge popularity in the mid 1990s. "At the beginning of the series," Shannon says, "the Stine and Pike books behaved themselves and we never experienced any oddities." It wasn't, as she later described, until the Goosebumps series published the tenth book that things began to go awry.

Shannon and her colleagues would enter the kids' section of the bookstore and find the books in small piles on the floor. "At first we believed that it was the customers playing pranks on us, as occasionally through the day the books would pile up on the floor." Then they noticed that even after the customers had left for the day and the staff had completed their ritualized rounds of tidying the entire store that the Goosebumps books would be in a pile again.

"We thought it odd but did not pay much attention to it until the same thing started happening in the morning. It was around that time that the Christopher Pike books joined in on the fun," she claims.

Shannon says that the staff did not have much choice except to joke about there being a ghost in the store, who seemed to enjoy playing practical jokes on them. Given that there was nobody in the store when the books were being piled up, there was no other explanation.

She described how they all examined the shelves, trying to determine if it could be the angle of the shelving that made the books consistently fall onto the floor. But even if that were the case, it wouldn't explain the strange manner in which the books had been piled up into adjacent piles, as if carefully placed by a pair of unseen hands. It also didn't explain why it was only books by these two authors and not others from the very same shelves.

When thinking about the events, Shannon just shrugged her shoulders and grinned, saying she had never experienced any-thing as odd or unexplainable since. Then, her intense brown eyes alight with that bookish thrill she wears so well, she went back to reminiscing about the fond memories she has of that cherished bookstore, the wonderful booksellers she worked with there, her love for slinging books, and sharing that intense personal passion for reading with so many great customers (and the resident ghost).

UNITED STATES OF AMERICA

KEROUAC'S FAVOURITE HAUNT
Haslam's Book Store
St. Petersburg, Florida

Booksellers are used to having authors come in and make a fuss if their latest book is not shelved face out, near eye level, and included in some sort of prominent display. The booksellers at Haslam's Book Store, though, have had to get used to the same sort of thing from an author who has been dead for decades.

A home-away-from-home for local authors as well as those from around the globe, Haslam's has always been a favourite haunt for those who court the written word. Among authors who regularly visited the store was famous American writer Jack Kerouac. In fact, he not only returned regularly to the bookshop during his life, but also from beyond the grave.

Kerouac, a writer and poet who is well known as a pioneer of the Beat Generation alongside writers like Allen Ginsberg and William S. Burroughs, moved to Florida in 1957 and resided in St.

Petersburg with his mother and third wife in the 1960s.[1] Haslam's was a regular hangout for Kerouac, who visited the bookstore to display his books and lecture on his personal philosophies. Occasionally, though, he would slip into the store with slightly more nefarious purposes. The owner at the time, Charles Haslam, is reported to have, on several occasions, had talks with Kerouac regarding his habit of re-arranging his books on the shelves. Eager to have his books at eye-level and facing out, Kerouac would regularly move his books to places that he felt were optimal for display.[2,3]

"Every author wants their books at eye level," says Ray Hinst, one of Haslam's current owners, "and so he would move his stuff. In those days there were no computers. We used to keep track visually and it screwed everything up all the time. He did it on a regular basis."[4]

After Kerouac's death in 1969 at the age of forty-seven, the writer is believed to have returned to the bookstore. Although his post-mortem visits are not as rude and unpleasant as they had been in the past, legends abound regarding the author's spirit continuing to move his books to more prominent display locations and flinging books off shelves.

Long time staff members and bookstore patrons report that at various times they have felt what might be the restless spirit of Jack Kerouac, have heard quiet, inexplicable, disembodied voices late at night, and on occasion actually witnessed a book slowly pop out from the shelf and fall to the ground, as if being pushed from the back. The feeling of being watched is also common and some reports include the feeling of a sudden cold breeze in the middle of the store, far from any door, almost as if there was something — or someone — brushing past them. Others report feeling a tap on their shoulder, even though there is nobody standing behind them.[5]

Although Hinst doesn't believe in ghosts himself, he has personally witnessed strange phenomenon that he can't explain.

"I was here late one night," Hinst said in an interview with local reporter Laura Kadechka, "I was doing some straightening over here and all of the sudden, boom, boom." Hinst looked down to see a collection of Kerouac's books on the floor.[6]

Other books occasionally tumble to the floor, and, during an 80th anniversary celebration at the store in December 2013, the *St. Petersburg Tribune* reported that in the middle of the reminiscences by bookstore staff and customers, a stack of children's books flew inexplicably from a display.[7]

"When you walk in the door you know this place is something different," Ray Arsenault, a local historian and co-director of the St. Petersburg Florida Studies Program at the University of South Florida, says, "and some strange things could happen here."[8]

Arsenault is not the only one. "As soon as you walk in, you feel like it's something special," said customer Tanya Santana in a 2011 interview with *10 News* reporter Laura Kadechka. "History is here. I love it."[9]

Sheila Cavallo, an Orlando-based medium, believes that more than a single ghost is present at Haslam's. She purports seeing a malevolent spirit of a man, approximately seventy years of age, with a bulbous nose, thick whiskers, and greyish, thinning hair, glaring at her. The ghost is not one who came to the bookstore naturally, but due to a renovation[10]: during their late-1970s expansion into the neighbouring People's Gas Company complex, perhaps Haslam's activated this once-dormant spirit.[11]

Paranormal group S.P.I.R.I.T.S. (a ghost-hunting society based in St. Petersburg) has conducted multiple investigations of the bookstore and has files containing photographs and video recordings of visual orbs. Paranormal investigators have also recorded drops in temperature, as much as fifteen to twenty degrees, as well as irregularly high electromagnetic field readings in particular sections of the store, particularly the do-it-yourself and home improvement areas.[12]

"We've had some odd occurrences in the store," Ray Hinst admitted to Tom Zucco, a *St. Petersburg Times* reporter. "The temperature seems to change in certain spots, and books have flown from the shelves."[13]

But Hinst goes on to say that they take it all "with a grain of salt," and jokes that the ghosts are welcome so long as they are well-behaved. Hinst says that he is more concerned with the living customers that come into their store. So whether you are attracted to Haslam's because of the rich history and culture, the unbeatable selection of new and used books, or just merely to soak in the ambiance of the spirits walking among the shelves, there's no doubt that when you walk through those doors, the experience will indeed be unique.

The largest new-and-used bookstore in Florida, Haslam's Book Store started four generations and over eight decades ago as a used book and newspaper shop. It carries hundreds of thousands of books, hosts multiple author readings and signings every month, and is, as stated by the *St. Petersburg Times*, "a Mecca for the city's book lovers and writers."[14]

Raymond Hinst, son of owners Suzanne Haslam and Ray Hinst, says that the store is not necessarily a reflection of his family, but of the community. "Everything that's in here came from your homes," Raymond said in an interview with the *St Petersburg Tribune* in December 2013. "You brought it in to us or called it in because you were interested in it. Everyone in this town made a store this big with all this amazing diversity and history, and you're still bringing more in."[15]

In 1933, John and Mary Haslam, who were both avid readers, took it upon themselves to start up a store that would provide readers with used magazines and books at bargain prices. With the Great Depression having entered its third year, money was in short supply, and local residents took advantage of two great offerings provided by the store. Those looking for information or escape could find affordable second-hand books and magazines to purchase; and those in need of money to keep food on the table could sell those same items to the bookstore.

After World War II, the bookstore moved into the hands of second-generation owners Charles and Elizabeth Haslam, who further diversified the selection of material, incorporating new books, technical manuals, bibles, children's books, and a complete line of new trade books in order to fulfill customer requests. In order to accommodate the growing selection (an offering that would eventually grow to between 300,000 and 400,000 titles) the store moved four times, settling at its current location at 2025 Central Avenue in St. Petersburg in 1966.[16, 17]

Charles and Elizabeth Haslam remained active as authors, booksellers, and advocates for reading and bookselling throughout their lives. Charles was the American Booksellers Association president from 1978 to 1980; Elizabeth contributed to the American Booksellers Association's *A Manual of Bookselling* and was an informal mentor to countless booksellers.

Charles died in the fall of 1983 from malaria, which was contracted on a visit to Africa at the age of seventy, and Elizabeth died at 94 in 2007. The two have been honoured by the Southern Independent Booksellers Alliance (SIBA) with the Haslam Award for Excellence in Independent Bookselling. Their spirit and passion continue to breathe life into the thirty-thousand-square-foot store.

THE TRAGIC STORY OF YOUNG MOLLY

The Off Campus Bookstore
(University of North Alabama)

Florence, Alabama

A t The Off Campus Bookstore near the University of North Alabama, visitors often see the ghost of a little girl alongside a puppy. While the origin of resident ghosts can usually only be guessed at, the girl's tragic story can be traced back to when the bookstore was a private home.

Molly was an eleven-year-old girl who lived in the house with her mother and father during the 1930s or early 1940s. She was a happy little girl but an only child and spent much of her time playing alone with her dolls in her room. When she expressed a feeling of loneliness to her parents, Molly's father went out and purchased a puppy for her.[18, 19]

The young girl was so enthralled with the dog that she played with it all day and snuggled in bed with it at night. The two were inseparable, and Molly had never been happier. Her parents were similarly pleased with the new puppy and delighted in the fact that their little girl had such a dear and adorable little friend.[20]

Things were fine for several days, until one horrifying evening when Molly's parents woke in the middle of the night to the sound of screaming was coming from Molly's room.[21] Mortified, they rushed into her room to discover that the dog had bitten the little girl. It wasn't clear if the dog had reacted to being rolled onto while it slept, or if it had acted out in the blurry haze of a bad dream, but after everybody had calmed down, they all managed to get back to sleep.[22]

Things continued on as normal, until both Molly and her dog began to show signs of illness.[23] Molly and the dog were diagnosed with rabies and had progressed too far too quickly for treatment to be effective. They both died shortly after the diagnosis.[24]

The legend surrounding Molly never explains what happened to her family, only that the house eventually was remodeled and became a fraternity. There are stories of frat boys seeing the ghost of a young girl gazing out the second-storey window, accounts of a young girl in a beautiful dress beckoning to visitors, and reports of the ghostly voice of a young girl asking people if they have seen her dog.[25, 26]

During a homecoming parade, a group of students recall waving at a cute little girl who was watching them from the second-floor balcony of the bookstore. Not realizing that it was the bookstore, they later asked who the cute little girl was that lived at the house and were shocked to learn that the admirer watching them from upstairs was none other than the ghost of little Molly.[27]

Bookstore employees say that Molly sometimes appears alone and sometimes appears with the ghost of her beloved little puppy. There have also been reports of candy missing from the bookstore shelves some mornings when staff arrive at the store.[28]

Debra Johnston Glass, author of the book *Skeletons on Campus: True Ghost Stories of Alabama Colleges and Universities*, conducts the Shoals Ghost Walk during the Halloween season every year. The bookstore is a recurring stop and several walkers on the tour have admitted to seeing Molly's ghost looking down longingly at them from the second-storey window. One tour member allegedly snapped a photo that appears to show the little girl standing in the corner.[29]

THE PORTAL

Bob's Beach Books

Lincoln City, Oregon

A s a bookseller, you never know who will come into your store. And if you are at Bob's Beach Books, you don't know who might never leave — at least not via conventional methods.

About two years ago on an afternoon not significantly different than any other, Diana Portwood was working in her store when an older couple came in. The cash desk was located on the right side of the entrance, so Diana had a clear view of all visitors as they entered and left her store.

"Good afternoon," she greeted them as they walked in. "Can I help you find anything?"

Diana casually observed the couple, who appeared to be in their mid-sixties, noting they were not unlike a lot of couples who came into the store. However, they were perhaps dressed a bit more conservatively than most people wandering into the beach-area store. The woman was wearing a sweater and a long skirt, while the man, with his sweater, elbow patches, white hair, and beard, struck Diana as the professorial type.

"No, thanks," the woman said. They walked past the front desk and went straight up the set of three steps into the back half of the store.

They were wandering around for about twenty minutes before Diana approached them again.

"Are you sure there's nothing I can help you find?" she asked. "Is there a certain book or type of book you were looking for?"

"Well," the woman said. "We're not exactly looking for a book. We're looking for the Portal."

"The Portal?"

"Yes, the Portal." The woman then explained that they had been doing research for years and determined that the Portal to Lemuria was here in Lincoln City.

"The Portal to Lemuria?" Diana asked.

"Exactly," the woman replied. "Lemuria. We have been following the energy and it has led us here. We are certain that the Portal is contained within a bookstore right here in this town. But we are having trouble finding it."

The woman mentioned that they were also considering trying the other bookstore located just a few miles down the road. But they were certain that the energy said the portal would be in this particular location.

Diana, having been surrounded by books her entire life, could certainly understand the intense allure that books might have. Why wouldn't a bookstore be the ideal place for a portal?

The woman thought that maybe the portal was under the stairs.

Speaking for the first time, the man wondered if they should perhaps give it another walk-around before checking out the area under the stairs.

"Well," Diana said, "just let me know if you need anything."

At that point, Diana turned and walked back to the cash desk to sort through some paperwork.

She never saw the couple again.

Bob's Beach Books, Lincoln City, Oregon.

There is no way, in such a small shop, that Diana could have missed seeing them leave. "They just disappeared, somewhere in the store. They didn't seem anything but normal," Diana said when I interviewed her in March 2014. She explained that their behaviour was not in the least erratic, that their speech and movements were all normal, and that they seemed most certainly sane, "except for their insistence that there was a portal in my bookstore," Diana laughed. "You never know *who* is going to walk into your bookstore."

Were the old couple investigators who had indeed discovered a special portal in Bob's Beach Books, drawn by a mystical energy that led them to a gateway to an ancient long-lost land known as Lemuria? Or, were the couple not even of this world, but two spectres joined in some beyond-this-life quest to find the plane of the afterlife?

Diana isn't sure. But she will never forget what they looked and sounded like, and in the two years since this incident occurred, has not yet seen them again.

THE HAUNTED POETRY BOOK

The Lady of the Lake by Sir Walter Scott
Ocala, Florida

If book lovers can avidly cling to their favourite books, never wanting to part with them, can the same be said for a ghost that latches on to one?

The Lady of the Lake is a narrative poem written by Sir Walter Scott in 1810 and something that, in its time, was tremendously influential. By the late twentieth century, the poem was virtually forgotten, and, two hundred years later, while still studied and celebrated by scholars, it has fallen out of popular discussion and general praise.[30]

One particular copy of this book, however, seems to have become the object of choice for one of the ghosts that resided in The Scott House in Ocala, Florida. Part of the larger property known as The Seven Sisters Inn Bed & Breakfast, the inn, which has claimed to be "The Most Haunted Bed and Breakfast" in Florida, has been featured on SciFi Channel's *Ghost Hunters*, and has as many as seven spirits taking residence there.[31]

When paranormal investigator Nancy Planeta accepted an invitation to investigate the locale in 2009, she never realized the keepsake she would end up possessing, or just how unique the experience would be.[32]

The owner had Nancy and her team stay in a room called "Sylvia's Room," which used to belong to Mrs. Elizabeth Scott. Nancy found herself immediately drawn to an 1893 American Book Company printing of the Sir Walter Scott poem *The Lady of the Lake*. She learned from the owner that the book was part of the original estate of the house and had been found in the attic. She immediately picked the book up and started leafing through it, before finally placing it back on the nightstand next to the bed.[33]

Later that evening when Nancy and her team were setting up their equipment in the upstairs loft, they decided to turn on the ceiling fans in order to get some relief from the stagnant heat. No sooner had the switch been flipped when something came flying off one of the fan blades striking Nancy in the head.[34]

It was the book *The Lady of the Lake*.[35]

Nancy shook her head at the book, laughed, and said out loud, "Funny. You're really funny; but knocking me out is not the way to get my attention."[36]

They proceeded to return, with the book, back down to Sylvia's room, believing that a spirit from that room was trying to communicate with them. But despite their best attempts, they received no positive results.[37]

So they moved on to other areas of the house and were kept busy with a miscellany of paranormal activity that they documented in EVP (Electronic Voice Phenomenon) and video recordings until almost 6:00 a.m., when they decided to pack it in.[38]

When Nancy arrived home and started unpacking, she found an unknown hitchhiker in her laptop bag. When she pulled her laptop out, something else fell out and onto her foot. It was the copy of *The Lady of the Lake*.[39]

Nancy immediately called the owner to let her know she had inadvertently removed the book from the premises and promised she would bring it right back. But the owner told Nancy to keep the book, figuring that the book had found its rightful way to the person who should have it. Though she found the sentiment a bit odd, Nancy had wanted to read the book anyway and so was happy to keep it.[40]

Despite finding its apparent rightful owner, the book, obviously still haunted with a playful spirit, continues to play a unique game of hide and seek with Nancy.[41]

"Every once in a while," Nancy said, "it will disappear from my desk in my bedroom, and reappear in the oddest places." She has found the book in her china cabinet, in the wastebasket, and even in her refrigerator.[42]

I never learned if she has had time to read the book like she had desired, but it's fun to imagine a book, or at least a spirit that is attached to a book, going to such lengths in order to continue to capture a potential reader's interest.

DEATH AND RESURRECTION OF THE BOOK HOUSE

The Book House

St. Louis, Missouri

The spirits of no less than three deceased persons haunt the original location of The Book House. The store's location has a long history: the original owner of the 1863 home was a ship captain by the name of George Keith. During the late 1800s the farmhouse operated as an inn, lodging a series of temporary boarders, and legend also has it that the building was, for a time, a brothel. At one point, the building was said to have been occupied by a doctor who ran a practice out of it, as well as a "dying room" — a hospital and morgue.[43]

One of the spiritual occupants is a ghost by the name of Valerie, a little red-headed girl, who was believed to have drowned in a well on the property. Employees and customers have heard Valerie giggling as she mischievously moves books around the store, walks around on the roof, levitates outside the second-storey windows, and occasionally turns the lights on and off. Visitors to the bookstore have reported the uncanny feeling of being watched, of having their clothes tugged on, and even bumping into an eerie young girl of about four or five years old.[44]

A darker spirit has also made an appearance at the bookstore, allegedly showing up in the dark of night. "The Dark Man," as he is referred to, is dressed all in black and has been encountered on the basement stairs. His presence is always associated with an overwhelming sense of dread and fear, as well as an intense chill in the air.[45]

Another ghost, known as "The Smoking Man," started showing up in 2002. He is believed to be the spirit of a man who owned a set of books donated to the bookstore from his estate. This gentleman has been seen walking around the store and smoking his pipe. The smell of the burning pipe was so bad once that employees called the fire department, believing that there was actually a fire in the store.[46]

The original location of The Book House.

Founded in 1986 by Michelle Barron and family-owned and-operated, The Book House in St. Louis was an iconic and respected community bookstore selling new, used, and unusual books, and was located in an historic Victorian house built in 1863.[47]

The bookstore, which held over 350,000 books acquired from hundreds of collections, auctions, and suppliers, was voted *Best of St. Louis* and *St. Louis A-List* winner for 2008, 2009, 2010, and 2013.[48]

After weathering the slings and arrows of an often uphill economy, even with a 20 percent increase in sales the year after a local Borders store closed down, and after surviving with three alleged ghosts haunting the building, the magic that sustained this exquisite gift to book lovers came crashing down.[49]

In the spring of 2013, owner Michelle Barron was given ninety days to vacate the building in order to demolish it and put up a 25,000-square-foot storage facility. Despite more than 650 people signing a petition to preserve the 150-year-old building, the family-owned business was served an eviction notice and forced to leave.[50]

Barron refused to give up and brought her cause to find and fund a new home for The Book House to the website Kickstarter.

"We were trying to find something iconic, something old and historic," Barron told reporter Lindsay Toler in a November 2013 *Daily Riverfront Times* article, "because that's kind of what we're known for."[51]

They searched long and hard and found a new space that Barron felt captured the friendly and historic atmosphere of their original location in a hundred-year-old building at 7352 Manchester Road, right in the heart of a wonderful community in a special historic district of the town of Maplewood, Missouri.[52]

In February of 2014, The Book House officially announced its re-opening, and on Tuesday, March 18 the official ribbon-cutting ceremony took place.[53, 54]

SOME BROWSE FOREVER

Browse Awhile Books

Tipp City, Ohio

Shadows playing peek-a-boo and toys moving as if by unseen children's hands are two of the eerie phenomena reported at Browse Awhile Books.

Customers of the bookstore have reportedly experienced ghostly voices, had books leap off shelves and onto their heads, and have even had ghosts physically touch them. The owner of the store also reports that toys left out for children to play with had moved all on their own.[55] Others report the feeling of being watched and followed, the sounds of mysterious footsteps and crashing sounds, shadows playing peek-a-boo, and books being thrown and moved.[56]

The bookstore has been featured in countless paranormal investigations and television programs such as *Haunted Collector*. In a recorded attempt to speak with the ghost, investigators were certain that they heard a child's voice speak the word "no." This was in response to the question of whether or not the ghost had meant to frighten people in the store.[57]

Some paranormal investigators have determined that the name of the child's ghost might be Caleb, and that he arrived at the bookstore attached to a book. The bookstore staff believe that many of the ghosts who haunt the premises have arrived in a similar fashion.[58]

Ghosts by the names of Charlie, Sam, Virgil, and James are allegedly the spirits of previous owners or tenants who died in the building over the years. The ghost Erika claimed to be the daughter of one of the previous owners, and Eliza apparently worked in the bakery that occupied the building in the 1950s. Other ghosts by the names of Becky Sue, Mike, and Ellen are also said to frequent the premises.[59]

DIG (Doorways Investigation Group) took a paranormal walkthrough video of the bookstore. It features a tour guide sharing a story about a woman who reported being slapped in one of the back rooms of the bookstore. It was later found out that the woman had been trying to steal a book at the time.[60] Could it be that one of the ghosts was protecting the store's inventory?

In January 2013, the Paranormal Answers Research Team (PART) posted a series of three videos, covering more than twenty minutes of investigation, attempting to document as many as fifteen different spirits that haunt the location. Apart from a strange series of voices that the cameras picked up, some of which could be heard by the investigators, investigator Kelly felt something holding onto her hand in the dark of the basement. Shortly after, team members claimed to have seen a white mist move toward Kelly just as she felt something hard brush against her.[61]

A popular location for ongoing investigations, Browse Awhile Books features regularly scheduled and bookable tours. If you are in the area and in the mood for an excellent selection of used books and mischievous spirits, make sure to stop by.

Built in 1872, Browse Awhile Books is a city block long and consists of two levels at 118 E. Main Street, Tipp City, Ohio. The building itself has been home to numerous businesses over the years, including a hardware store, a grocery store, a billiards hall, a bakery, and a produce shop.[62]

THE GRIEVING GHOST OF GREENE'S

Greene's Antiques/Barber's Book Store

Fort Worth, Texas

A t one time in its history, the building that housed Barber's
Bookstore was a busy (and shady) hotel in what was once
an infamous red-light district. The back staircase of what used
to be the Adam's Hotel was the supposed location of at least one
ghost that continued to haunt the vicinity long after the hotel
closed its doors. As legend tells, a young woman and her male
lover, who were planning to run away together, had been staying
in Room 11. When the girl's father learned about them, and the
fact that his daughter worked as an entertainer at the hotel, he
was so enraged that he ambushed the young man and shot him
dead as he walked out of the hotel room. [63, 64]

The distraught girl, unable to live without him, killed herself,
although accounts differ on the manner by which she took her
own life. One account has her immediately committing suicide

in the hotel room, while another says she was so grief-stricken that she went up to the roof and launched herself off the top of the building.[65, 66]

Years later, books from the shelves of Barber's Book Store used to drop onto the floor from their place on the shelves for no reason, and witnesses reported hearing the sound of turning pages when nobody was around. The sound of footsteps echoing on the stairs was another disturbing sound, and some people reported being brushed by an unseen presence while smelling the odour of perfume in the vicinity.[67]

Mitchel Whitington wrote about his personal experiences visiting the bookstore owners Dwight and Sheila Greene in his 2003 book, *Ghosts of North Texas*.

One of the first stories the Greenes shared with Whitington had to do with the girl from Room 11 who took her own life. When a female merchant later rented that same room to conduct her antiquing business, she discovered that, day after day, some unseen force was pushing the cups and saucers that she had carefully placed on the shelf onto the floor.[68]

The grieving ghost of the young woman was apparently upset by the presence of anyone or anything else in that room. Anyone, that is, other than the love that her father had so cruelly and quickly taken away from her.

Although it closed in 1997, with all stock and inventory liquidated in 1998, the building that housed Barber's Book Store (and the shop-within-a-shop, Greene's Antiques), was originally constructed between 1908 and 1910 and was remodelled in the 1930s with an Art Deco facade. [69, 70]

READING IN THE DARK

Mary Reed Hall, University of Denver
Denver, Colorado

You might recall the oft-repeated motherly advice that reading in the dark is bad for your eyes. But that doesn't seem to bother one particular female ghost at the University of Denver. In fact, she seems to prefer the dark for her reading comfort.

Shortly after receiving a $500,000 donation from Mary D. Reed, planning for construction of the Mary Reed Hall began on the University of Denver campus. A cornerstone of the older part of campus, the red-brick, 126-foot central tower of the building was designed to reflect a modified collegiate gothic. A Renaissance Room, a treasure trove for students to browse and discover books, including a collection of rare books and manuscripts, contains a portrait of Mary Reed that hangs in honour of her generosity.[71, 72]

The portrait of this university benefactor doesn't seem to be the only thing that maintains a sentry-like vigil inside the building, though. Reports of strange happenings and ghostly sightings abound, and many believe that the phenomena stem from the spirit of Mary Reed, as well as a few additional spirits.

One of the first tales regarding a ghostly sighting involves a young woman who was walking around the building, waiting for her boyfriend to finish some late-night work. When she entered the Renaissance Room, she discovered a woman sitting in a chair in the dark, apparently reading. When the lights came on, the strange woman looked up, then stood and began to approach the girl. The student immediately fled the room, found her boyfriend, and they left the building. After they got into his car, she looked up to the windows of the room and watched the lights turn off as they drove away. Apparently, the strange apparition wasn't finished reading in the dark.[73]

When the Penrose Library was built in 1972, the Mary Reed Building became home to administrative staff, including payroll, chancellor, and provost staff members.[74] Pat Kavanaugh, an employee from the university's payroll office, told University of Denver newspaper *Clarion* reporter, Charles Ng, that lights often went on and off late at night in the Mary Reed Building, even with newly installed bulbs. "They can blame it on old electricity," Kavanaugh said. "But I think they [the ghosts] like the dark."[75]

There are further stories about ghosts in different parts of the building. Mary's ghostly companions include alumna Margery Reed, who died in 1925, and Marcella Miller Du Pont, a poet who is said to haunt the DuPont room, a study room inside the Mary Reed Building. It was dedicated in 1967 in honour of Marcella's family for her donation and her desire to see "a room where students or scholars could work in pleasant, comfortable surroundings." Du Pont died in September 1985. [76, 77]

A story not unlike the one reported in the Renaissance Room involves a young man who switched on the light in the DuPont

Room to discover a woman in an old-fashioned dress sitting in a high-backed leather chair, reading. She not only looked up at the young man, but stood from the reading chair and greeted him. He didn't return the greeting, instead quickly exiting the room, leaving the light on. Shortly after he left, the light went back off.[78]

Custodians in the building have also reported seeing an elderly woman sitting and reading in the dark late in the night, and there have been reports of a particular chair in the old library feeling warm, as if someone had just been sitting in it, even if the chair had been empty for hours.[79, 80] Other reports tell of a transparent figure seen reading or sometimes on the staircase, of books flying off the shelves, and of being shoved by an invisible force.[81]

Glenna Leff, another payroll department staff member, spoke about a "definite cold area" to *Clarion* staff, and shared stories about staff members feeling cold spots in various locations, as well as being inexplicably pushed from behind by unseen forces.[82]

The director of custodian services, Alfredo Abad, says that stories about ghostly sightings and experiences of being pushed from behind get passed from employee to employee, and that some of his staff refuse to work alone in the Mary Reed Building. He shared the tale of a custodian who was continually shoved while trying to lock up the building, only to find nobody there every time he turned. Custodial staff have, in fact, determined that all cleaning work be completed in the building prior to 10:00 p.m., which is usually when the building begins to empty.

That way, the ghost, or ghosts, who prefer reading in the quiet darkness, can read undisturbed through the night.

NAT THE NATIONAL TREASURE

Amarillo Natatorium Bookstore

Amarillo, Texas

The thought of pairs of ghosts gliding gracefully in spectral form on an otherwise empty dance floor can seem both frightening and hauntingly beautiful. While some might find it eerie, others might consider it a fitting homage to the past.

Affectionately nicknamed "The Nat" since its inception in July 1922, the Amarillo Natatorium first opened to the public as an open-air swimming pool. In 1923, the building was enclosed so that the pool could be used year round and, in 1926, the building was converted into a 10,000-square-foot dance hall.[83, 84]

In 1994, The Nat was placed on the National Register of Historic Places and, a year later, it was deemed a Texas Historical Landmark. The second floor was renovated into an antique mall and the old Nat Café on the main floor was turned into a bookstore. The old ballroom is occasionally still rented out for special community events and concerts.[85]

Various spiritual manifestations have been reported in The Nat, including ghostly couples gliding around the dance floor whenever a new band is performing in the old ballroom space. A woman in a 1930s-era dress has been spotted walking around with an obvious wine stain on her front, seemingly in a very jovial mood and extremely pleased to be part of the festivities.[86]

In her book *Ghosthunting Texas*, author April Slaughter recalls visiting The Nat in order to gain a bit more insight into the building's colourful past and ghostly present. Meeting with bookstore owners Aaron Baker and Sarah Stone, Slaughter felt immediately at ease when entering the quaint little bookstore, particularly after being greeted by George, the bookstore's resident cat.[87]

While there, Slaughter interviewed a gentleman by the name of Branden Mann, who leased and managed the Nat Ballroom, which is accessed through the back of the bookstore. Mann explained that he had gotten so used to the strange and inexplicable noises over the years that he had stopped paying much attention to them.[88]

"On one particular occasion," Mann explained, "I heard what I thought was the sound of a woman speaking in the same mumbling voice you would hear on a Charlie Brown cartoon. I couldn't understand what was being said, but I definitely knew that someone was speaking close-by."[89]

The Nat has been a popular site for paranormal enthusiasts, and at one session eerie recordings (known as electronic voice phenomenon, or EVP) captured the melodic singing of an unseen woman and the ghostly sounds of a solitary drum.[90]

Sudden fluctuations in temperature have been reported in the building, and disembodied voices have also been recorded in particular spots within the bookstore. Some of the paranormal investigators have been frustrated with the fact that their recording equipment encountered inexplicable power failures, almost as if the ghosts were not at all comfortable with being recorded or having their privacy violated.[91] Obviously, they wish to continue their ghostly dance in peace.

THE GHOST OF HARRIET HASKELL

Reid Memorial Library (Lewis and Clark Community College, Godfrey Campus)

Alton, Illinois

Some people are so dedicated to something in life that it is easy to imagine them continuing their chosen work even after they die. Such is the case with Harriet Haskell, whose presence continues post-life at a campus that she dedicated so much of her life to.

Born in 1835 in Waldoboro, Maine, Harriet Haskell became the first female headmaster of the Franklin School in Boston. In 1867, she became the new principal at Monticello Seminary, where she stayed for four decades. In her reign there she was acclaimed as one of the Midwest's greatest early educators, making Monticello one of the most respected female institutions in the United States.[92, 93]

Lewis and Clark College was founded on the grounds of the Monticello school in 1970, and the old school chapel is now the college library.[94] But there are those who believe that Haskell's spirit still lives on at her beloved campus. The legends began when, at the oldest building on the campus, lights in empty rooms would turn on by themselves, water would run in vacant bathrooms, and the steam-operated elevator in the administration building would mysteriously travel between floors in the middle of the night, much to the befuddlement of the security guards who witnessed it.[95]

Reports of sightings of Harriet Haskell's spirit were also spread through the halls. Some of the most popular ones were perpetuated by new students, frightened into behaving with tales of Miss Haskell's ghost patrolling the dorm hallways at night. But the one place on campus where she is most consistently seen is the old Monticello chapel, which was converted into the Reid Memorial Library.[96]

Sightings of Haskell's ghost are often preceded by an overwhelming scent of lilac, a fragrance she was known to wear. One such encounter was reported by a librarian who was straightening magazines in a corner of the library one evening when she spotted a tall woman in an old-fashioned dress standing before the main desk. Just as she was about to ask the woman if she needed help finding something, the woman faded away.[97]

Another librarian, also working alone, reported feeling someone touch her on the shoulder from behind. When she turned in response, there was nobody there. Returning to her work, she felt another tap, this time on her arm. Again, when she turned, there was nobody there. Though that particular librarian didn't believe in ghosts, she was positive that something or someone was with her in the library that evening.[98]

One Halloween evening, at the end of an on-location broadcast in the library, a student DJ, who professed to being skeptical about the existence of a ghost in the library, swore that on two separate occasions he felt the distinct impression of a hand being placed on his shoulder, despite being the only person in the room at the time.[99]

Troy Taylor, author of *Haunted Alton: History and Hauntings of the Riverbend Region*, recounts one of the most chillingly convincing tales from the college. It involved maintenance staff and a security guard who were attempting to assist a young woman who had gotten stuck between floors in the library elevator. The young woman was extremely upset and kept asking for help, before beginning to cry. The security guard continued speaking with her, doing his best to keep her calm while the maintenance staff worked on the electrical panel in an attempt to get the elevator unstuck. When they finally succeeded in getting the elevator moved and the doors opened, they discovered there was nobody inside the elevator car![100]

Harriet Haskell's imagination, wit, and sharp sense of humour were adored by her students, and it was said that she could anticipate any tricks that the young students attempted to play on her because, as a young girl herself, she had been known as the "holy terror" of her family.[101]

An early advocate for sports for women, Haskell believed that if young women were well-off physically, they would also be emotionally and morally fit.[102] Similarly, she was able to make the course of religious studies so intriguing and interesting that a group of local boys not attending the school attended the instruction willingly.[103]

One Christmas, in order to lift the spirits of some of the young ladies who did not travel home for the holidays, but, instead, stayed at the school, she dressed up as Santa Claus. Unfortunately, because she strayed too close to the lit candles on the Christmas tree, her fake beard caught on fire, and the left side of her face was severely burned. (This is why the archival paintings of Miss Haskell only ever show her right profile.)[104]

A devastating fire in 1888 left nothing but a pile of smouldering ruins and the blackened shell of the school tower. But in the throes of the disaster, Harriet Haskell stood in the dormitory doorway, calmly surveying the students, carefully inspecting each girl as she fled from the building by ensuring that they were properly dressed and presentable.[105, 106]

Haskell's rare book collection and piano managed to be saved by a group of arriving volunteers who realized that the building was a lost cause, but that some of the contents and personal belongings could be saved.[107] Haskell, however, seemed more concerned with the fate of her beloved school, and as the young women departed the school with what few possessions they had loaded into trunks, they could see her standing on the college lawn, silently staring at the charred remains of the school.

Haskell's determination for her school would not be quelled. Shortly after the fire, she undertook a fundraising campaign, collecting thousands of dollars and beginning the launch of a new building that was known as Caldwell Hall.[108]

Although Haskell never married nor had daughters of her own, she did raise two nieces, and many students left the school with the feeling that Miss Haskell loved them like they were her own children. When she died in 1907, her students (known as the Haskell Girls), were deeply grieved. Former students from across the United States travelled to attend her funeral, and still many others, who were not able at attend in person, sent flowers and cards.[109, 110]

A book entitled *Harriet Newell Haskell: A Span of Sunshine Gold*, documenting Harriet Newell Haskell's life, was published in 1908 by Emily Gilmore Alden, and opens with the dedication to "Those who loved her much and long by One who loved her more and longer." The book is described by the author as "neither obituary notice nor eulogy," but rather as a "freehand character sketch of one so electrically alive that it seemed impossible for death to claim her. Indeed she yet lives — her potent influence the sunshine-gold that gilds to-day the towers of her new Monticello."[111]

SPELLBINDING STORIES

Spellbinding Tales

Alameda, California

While no longer in business, Spellbinding Tales, an independently owned and operated bookstore in what used to be a one-hundred-year-old railroad station, continues to live on in the many stories of ghostly encounters that took place there.[112]

After witnessing a rocking chair moving, from a spot in the middle of the room to a spot closer to the window, as well as banging, eerie voices, and the feeling that she was never alone in the store, former bookstore proprietor Karen Zimmerman contacted a group of paranormal investigators to come for a visit. Two groups (Ghost Trackers and Spirits-Speak) joined forces and visited the bookstore to perform a joint investigation.[113]

Apart from the rocking chair rocking by itself and a dark figure encountered on the stairs, the investigators discovered a series of lights flashing in the upper corners of the room, as well as a series of odd EVP (electronic voice phenomenon) recordings.[114]

Debby Constantine, one of the investigators from Spirits-Speak, was alone in the loft of the bookstore when she felt the overwhelming sensation of two distinct female entities rushing at her with every intent of forcing her to leave.[115] She also reported that during the day, when the bookstore was occupied with customers, the spirits she sensed moved out of the main bookstore area and hid away in the unoccupied apartments above the bookstore, as if trying to avoid the intruders.[116]

Debby's husband, Mark, reported feeling a heavy, thick negative energy when he was ascending the stairs, as if there was something trying desperately to express that he was not welcome there.[117]

Walt Baker, an investigator from West Virginia, also visited the store, and he took a photograph showing a concave mirror displaying a series of odd splotchy smudges, as if something — or someone — had been pressing up against it. The mirror, which was installed ten feet up and had never been touched, had previously been spotless.[118]

Zimmerman, the former bookstore owner, who went on to pen a book about ghost stories, was quoted in a 2008 *San Jose Mercury News* article, speaking about her old store.

"It's near a former train station," Zimmerman said, speculating that the ghosts that haunted the shop may have been from train accidents that took place nearby.[119]

THE MANY LIVES OF CARNEGIE LIBRARY

Carnegie Library/Trans-Allegheny Books

Parkersburg, West Virginia

An abandoned library spent ten years collecting dust before a bookstore moved in — is it any surprise that a few spirits started to call the building home?

In 1904, Andrew Carnegie provided $34,000 to fund the building of the Carnegie Library, a two-storey, L-shaped building in the Classical Revival style. It was one of almost three thousand such libraries that the philanthropist donated funding for.[120, 121, 122] The library boasted several reading rooms with huge, ornate fireplaces; a wrought iron circular staircase with brass handrail in the back of the building; and dynamic, hand-carved wooden staircases in the building's front. With a tile floor entryway, a glass floor, and a lavish stained-glass window in the back, the building provided a regal home for books, and, perhaps, for ghostly visitors.[123]

The library was operational until 1976, and sat unused for almost ten years before it was re-opened as a used bookstore called Trans-Allegheny Books.[124] The bookstore, owned by Joe Sakach, boasted half a million books and was the largest used bookstore in West Virginia. That alone would have made it a unique and desirable attraction, but the bookstore cranked it up a notch by embracing the legends of the ghosts that resided within.

The old website, mostly devoted to ghost tours rather than books, contained a header reading "Trans Allegheny Books, Inc. Introduces: Haunted Library Ghost Hunts!" along with the teaser: "Want to Spend Some Time In a Real Haunted Bookstore? What About Meeting Up With a Few Fantastic Phantoms?"[125]

Further text outlines the bookstore's ghostly proposition: private ghost hunts costing $250 for up to twenty-five people.

> Come on a private ghost hunt in an actual haunted building that dates back to the bygone days of the oil & gas era of Parkersburg, West Virginia!
>
> Built in 1905, the Parkersburg Carnegie Library building is the now home of Trans Allegheny Books, West Virginia's largest used bookstore! A wrought iron and brass spiral staircase, stained glass window, and hand-carved oak staircase and mantles link the past to the present and evoke the seductiveness of early 20th century Parkersburg.
>
> Ghost hunters & psychics proclaim the store has at least five primary spirits; three are women, another a child and also a man. The small girl (seen wearing a white bonnet) has been sighted on the wooden stairs leading to the second floor of the bookstore. Customers have actual[ly] tripped over her playing on the steps!

Many visitors claim to have seen a dapper older gentleman wearing a brown jacket and derby hat browsing the second floor, as well. There are even reports the bookstore is haunted by the ghost of a local newspaper reporter who was tragically murdered in her home on nearby Avery Street in the 1980s. The reporter spent a great deal of time in the old Carnegie Library and it was a second home to her.

Paranormal investigators have captured pictures of the spirits inside the bookstore — so convincing was the evidence of ghosts inside Trans Allegheny bookstore that it helped land the investigators a job with the television show "Scariest Places on Earth!"

Book your private Ghost Hunt now![126]

Theresa Racer, a paranormal investigator and historical researcher, outlines in her blog, *Theresa's Haunted History of the Tri-State*, a fascinating summary of the many legends that have been shared about the building's spirits. Racer says that no less than five different apparitions have been noted in the location and that books have been seen flying off the shelves, overhead lamps have been known to sway for no good reason, lights have mysteriously flickered on and off, and disembodied footsteps have been heard echoing in the halls.[127]

Racer describes the various apparitions, including a little girl in a white bonnet who appears to be approximately eight years old and is regularly seen either sitting on the third step or playing on the front wooden staircase leading to the second floor. Customers have reported accidentally tripping over a child they encountered on this staircase, only to realize that there was nobody there.[128]

The second floor boasted a dapper older man who was named "Henry" by visiting psychics. Henry is often seen in a brown jacket and wearing a derby hat. Another middle-aged male apparition is often seen in the World History section of the bookstore, always examining the shelves as if intently searching for some missing book.[129]

The fourth apparition is said to be that of a reporter for the *Parkersburg Sentinel* by the name of Betty Samuels, who was murdered in 1989 in her home by another woman named Janice Diers. Diers had been dating Betty's son Hunter and was apparently upset with the interference that Samuels posed in their relationship. Diers used her own key to Samuels's house and, according to police, confronted her in the upstairs bedroom and stabbed her three times. Samuels, who spent much of her time in the library before it had closed, is believed to have returned to the building after her death.[130, 131]

The bookstore is also home to at least one ghost cat. The spectral feline is said to have wandered and stalked along bookshelves, quickly disappearing behind them or simply vanishing when approached or looked at directly.[132]

While the building is currently empty once again, the spiritual inhabitants mean it will never be completely abandoned.

When bookstore owner Joe Sakach died in April 2010, speculation about the future of Trans-Allegheny Books and of the building began again, until the bookstore planned to hold a three-day liquidation sale in October of that year and close its doors for good. An injunction order prohibiting the sale of the bookstore's inventory was filed, preventing the sale almost as soon as it had started, and spiralling the legacy of the location into a stalemate position.[133, 134]

At the time of this writing, the building, at 725 Green Street, is a mere ghost of what it once was, standing vacant, un-used, and neglected by time. As history shows, however, it stood for almost ten full years between closing as a library and re-opening as a bookstore. Within that same time period (1982), it was listed on the National Registry of Historic Places, so rumours of its current death might be, as Mark Twain so eloquently said, "greatly exaggerated." The building was left vacant for a long period of time before coming back to new life, which means there is still a chance that the building itself will again find a robust new opportunity. Hopefully, people will once again be able to walk through the hallowed halls of Carnegie's great donation, and this former library and bookstore will breathe new life and vitality into the local cultural community of Parkersburg.

SMILE, YOU'RE ON GHOST CAMERA!

Willard Library

Evansville, Indiana

Established in 1885, Willard Library is the oldest public library building in the state of Indiana, but it is much more well-known as the home of "The Grey Lady of Willard Library," and the first library ever to install a live "Ghost Cam."

The first appearance of "The Grey Lady" occurred in 1937. As was his routine, the library custodian trekked through the snow on a cold winter morning at 3:00 a.m. in order to fire up the furnace and load it with coal to ensure the building was heated for the day. The furnace was located in the basement near what is today the children's department of the library. Moving through the dark, deserted hallways with his flashlight, on his way to the furnace room, he was startled to discover a figure standing quietly in the dark. It was a woman in a long, grey dress, a grey shawl, and grey veil. She was even wearing grey shoes. The custodian was so startled by this vision that he dropped his flashlight. A few seconds later, the woman vanished, leaving him alone again in the cold and quiet basement. The custodian reportedly quit his job shortly after, terrified about bumping into this eerie specter again.[135]

Joan Elliot Parker, special collections librarian, reported an unexplainable occurrence in the basement restroom. She had entered, locked the door, and gone into a stall. While she was in the stall, a pair of faucets began to run, despite the fact that the door was locked and nobody else was in the restroom with her. She left the stall and turned the faucets off, confused about how they could have started to run on their own.[136]

Longtime children's librarian Margaret Maier, who worked at the library for over fifty years, was reported to have had the most frequent encounters with the ghost. Recollecting her very first visit by the ghost in the 1950s, her description matched that of the custodian who had first encountered the spirit. She described the ghost as a woman dressed in a long shirt and blouse, with a grey shawl wrapped around her shoulders. Maier saw the woman standing among the bookshelves in an adjacent aisle, but she disappeared into thin air shortly after being observed.[137]

Maier reported that, having seen the ghost so many times and having worked in such close proximity with the spirit for so long, she and the Grey Lady had formed a special bond. The connection between the two was so great that during a remodelling of the children's department, which completely closed that section of the library, the ghost seemed to have followed her home. Maier and her sister claimed that they had seen the same ghost reported in the library floating through their living room and ascending the staircase. The ghost apparently remained there until after the remodelling was over, when it appeared to return to the library.[138, 139]

Numerous stories have been told about books falling off the shelves on their own in the basement children's department. At one time, a parent called to complain about her kindergarten child suffering nightmares about ghosts after her class visited the library, where staff shared some tales about the Grey Lady with them. After that, a library director instructed staff to stop talking to patrons about the ghost of the Grey Lady, or even admit that she existed when questioned. A few days after that, when a patron asked Assistant Children's Librarian Anita Glover about the ghost, she replied: "If she was here, she's not here anymore." No sooner had the words left Glover's mouth than a book entitled *Betsey's Wedding*, featuring a woman in a long, flowing wedding dress (not unlike the dress the Grey Lady was often reported wearing) fell to the floor at the feet of the two women, as if to demonstrate that the Grey Lady was indeed still present. After a short pause where the two women just stared at the book at their feet, Glover said, "Well, perhaps I'm mistaken.[140, 141]

Reports of a ghost (or ghosts) in the library are not limited to the basement. The Grey Lady of Willard Library has also been seen, felt, or heard on the first and second floors.

Although not much ghostly activity occurs on the first floor of the library, Louise Carpenter, thought to be the Grey Lady, has a presence on that floor, with a photo of her hanging on a wall. One time, during a paranormal investigation of the library by a pair of ghost hunters, one of them paused in front of the painting and commented on the fact that the woman wasn't at all attractive. The same investigator reported being overcome with an unsettled feeling for the rest of her time in the library, potentially because she had offended Louise.[142]

When a custodian got onto the elevator on the first floor in the early hours one particular morning, he was frustrated by the fact that, no matter which buttons he pressed, the car would not move. After several unsuccessful attempts, he said aloud: "I want to go down!" and the elevator started to comply. Employees working the night shift at the Berry Plastics building across the way reported seeing the Willard's elevator moving up and down all through the night. A library patron also reported encountering the Grey Lady during a solo elevator ride.[143]

A local meteorologist in the process of setting up an early morning shoot on the second floor witnessed several books sliding off a shelf, but as this was before the cameras were rolling, it was only recorded through word-of-mouth.[144]

Children's Librarian Rhonda Mort recounted a time during a meeting in the Bayard Room on the second floor of the library that she felt unbearably cold while sitting in a particular chair. The intense feeling of cold became so uncomfortable that she had to leave in order to get warm again. When she returned later, attempting to point out that chair to the library director, it was no longer where she had sat in it. Furthermore, the director said that to his personal knowledge no chair matching the description she gave had ever been a part of the library.[145]

Other reports of the Grey Lady include women feeling their hair or earrings being fondled while they are browsing through the stacks, and the sound of footsteps down empty corridors. One police officer reported seeing a female figure in the upstairs window, while his partner and the library director were inside the building responding to a night-time security alarm — the only two people in the building. The Grey Lady has also been associated with a strong lilac or lavender scent in the air.

Various paranormal groups have visited the library to investigate reports of the ghost, and every October the library sponsors annual Fright Night ghost tours that have become so popular that hundreds of visitors come through its doors.

In an intriguing move to capture the imagination of visitors both near and afar, the library has made finding and spotting the Grey Lady an interactive activity. On October 15, 1999, they installed the world's first Ghost Cam in three separate spots in the library. In the first two weeks of the Ghost Cam's operation, over two million visitors logged on to the library's website to try to catch a glimpse. Both *www.libraryghost.com* and *www.willardghost.com* were both set up with unique views of the webcams so that, day or night, virtual visitors could scan and submit screen captures of strange images that they have spotted.[146]

Greg Hager, Willard Library

Historic image of Willard Library.

Who Was the Grey Lady?

Designed by James and Merritt Reid, the Victorian Gothic Willard Library was designed for "the use of the people of all classes, races, and sexes, free of charge forever." But the library isn't known for its stature or the wonderfully long legacy it has held for serving the local community.[147, 148]

Willard Carpenter wanted to leave a lasting legacy in the town of Evansville. A well-known pioneer and philanthropist, Carpenter dreamed of building a college and naming it Willard College. He became fixated on using that name after being inspired by the Emma Willard School in Troy, New York.[149]

Despite his generosity, Carpenter had amassed a considerable fortune that he had been intending on using to create the college. Unfortunately, when a few dealings left him with a slight loss of fortune, combined with the down-turned real estate market, Carpenter turned his focus on a different institution that was about learning and would benefit the community.[150]

On August 23, 1876, Willard wrote a letter to the library trustees regarding his intent "in the well-grounded hope that such an institution may become useful toward the improvement of the moral and intellectual culture of the inhabitants of Evansville, and collaterally to those of the State of Indiana; and also toward the enlargement and diffusion of a taste for the fine arts."[151]

The groundbreaking for the library was scheduled for May 1877 and by the first anniversary of Carpenter's letter to the trustees, the stone foundation had been completed. That was followed by a series of construction delays, and it wasn't until 1882 that work on the building resumed. By 1883, Carpenter was eighty years old and, enthusiastic to see the building completed, actually participated in the work on the building, hauling wheelbarrows and scaling up to the framework roof.[152]

In late October of 1883, Carpenter suffered a paralyzing stroke and died on November 3.[153] Although he was generous with the community, he was apparently not as generous with his own family. Most of his fortune, he had decided, was going to public charity and not to his three children, Louise, Marcia, and Albert.[154]

Louise was most unhappy at the situation and engaged in a turn-of-the-century lawsuit against the library, attempting to gain back the fortune her father had given away. She tried to demonstrate that her father was not of sound mind when he made the donation, but despite her attempts and vehement protests, she lost the lawsuit and any claim that she had to the property or the holdings of the library.[155, 156]

Some say that Carpenter held a grudge with this lost family fortune, a grudge that she took with her to the grave, and that is whom many believe haunts the library in the spectral form of "The Grey Lady." Louise died in 1908, twenty-nine years before the first reported sighting. While some visiting psychics have identified the ghost as Louise, others described the ghost as being overwhelmed by a sense of loss that perhaps has something to do with a child and a nearby body of water.[157]

ALL GHOSTS WANT
SOME PEACE OF MIND

Peace of Mind Books

Tulsa, Oklahoma

Visitors of Peace of Mind Books have expressed that they feel an undeniable energy that seems to surround them the minute they step inside. It's not just the metaphysical artifacts or the collection of books on witchcraft, demonology, and the supernatural that they're talking about, though.[158]

The bookstore, still in operation, was originally located on Cherry Street in an old two-storey building that was once a hotel. Employees working in the original location reported a ghostly presence that seems to lend a powerful energy to the place. They have also noted strange things happening in the building, such as doors slamming, items being moved or flying off of the shelves as if struck by extreme force, books relocating themselves in a mysterious fashion, and ghostly apparitions.[159]

One might expect a little more paranormal activity in a

bookshop that specializes in the metaphysical and supernatural, but it still makes the employees uneasy. It's one thing to chat with customers about intriguing unexplainable phenomenon and quite another to be working alone in the store and seeing eerie shadows flittering about from the corner of your eye. And it's difficult enough picking up books after customers, never mind some unseen presence that seems to delight in shifting books around.

Since their move to the new location, there have been no reports by either staff members or customers about any strange supernatural goings-on. But one can be assured that, since the bookstore is filled with open minds dedicated to creating balance between mind, body, and spirit, if there ever is something spiritual lingering in the air, it will certainly be sensed and appreciated.

With over fifty thousand books on topics ranging from Astrology to Zoroastrianism, Peace of Mind Books in Tulsa, Oklahoma boasts the nation's largest collection of metaphysical books. The store also hosts classes and workshops on a wide variety of topics, such as meditation, yoga, nutrition, and mythology, and Tarot readings. The store also carries more than 175 different herbs, as well as stones, runes, and other metaphysical objects.[160, 161]

The bookstore has now relocated to its current address at 1401 East 15th Street. Hosted by their parent company, the Church of Holistic Science, Peace of Mind Books operates on the second floor and continues to specialize in unique, rare, and hard-to-find items, all dedicated to enlightenment.

A GHOST CALLED LOLA
Bridgeport Public Library
Bridgeport, Connecticut

L ibrarians are often known to provide out-of-this-world support and assistance to those who walk through their doors.
But at one library in Connecticut, there's an out-of-this-world
presence providing some help of her very own.

Staff have reported that the library is home to a friendly and
helpful ghost named Lola, who roams the historical stacks of the
sixth and seventh floors. Except, according to a written report
by Library Administrator Michael A. Gorlick, Lola sometimes
manages to get further afield in the building.[162]

In February 2006, Gorlick was called by the library's alarm
monitoring service just as he was about to go to bed. The alarm
at the main library had gone off. Gorlick said he would meet the
police there. Approximately ten minutes later, when he pulled
into the parking lot at the back of the building, he noticed that

all of the lights on the fifth floor were turned on. When he got in through the back door, he saw displayed on the alarm panel that the garage door was open. He walked through the building, confirmed that the door was indeed open, closed it, and then moved on to the fifth floor, where he proceeded to ensure that there was nobody in the building before turning off all of the lights.

He then cleared the alarm panel and waited for the police to show up. After thirty minutes, he decided they were not going to arrive, so he returned home. This was at approximately 11:00 p.m.

The next morning, the night custodian, who had remained in the building after Gorlick left the night before, mentioned that he had to close the garage door because he had found it open and wasn't able to set the alarm.

Even more odd, Gorlick learned that the library maintenance manager had been called just before midnight and arrived at the library to find three police cars, one parked out front and two parked around back. The garage door was open and he could see lights going on in the building as the police made their way through a check of the interior.

When the maintenance manager arrived at the sixth floor, he called out to the police so as not to startle them. But they had already been startled by odd noises they kept hearing during the search through the stacks. They had allegedly heard the sound of pages being turned, although they found no physical presence to support that noise. The police and the maintenance manager cleared the building, reset the alarm, and left.

Another phone call at 5:30 a.m. woke the maintenance manager. When he arrived, the garage door was again open, this time only by about a foot, and was in the process of closing. He noticed, when looking inside the library's delivery van, that the red light on the garage-door opener was on, indicating it was in the process of operating the door. At that point, just as the door completed closing, the manager called out: "All right, Lola, if you really are here, make the door open!"

Immediately, the door started to open. At that point, he took the batteries out of the remote control.

The issues with the garage door seemed to have ceased at that point.

Gorlick expresses the fact that, for the most part, stories about Lola involve the ghost actually being helpful, just like she was when she responded to the maintenance manager's request. In fact, she is known by staff for actually helping them find missing items.[163]

Being known as a helpful ghost fits in quite nicely with the library's mission to make a positive difference in the community. If only more ghosts could be so pleasant to work alongside.

The Bridgeport Public Library serves as the principal library for the City of Bridgeport, the most densely populated, largest municipality in Connecticut, with a population of 130,000 residents speaking as many as sixty different languages. The library offers exhibits featuring local artists; cultural programs for all ages focusing on art, literature, and music; and suburb historical collections; as well as a genealogy department that attracts visitors from all over the globe.[164]

Officially founded in 1881, the library opened at the corner of Main and John Street in a building donated by Catherine Burroughs Pettingill with a bequest note that desired the gift to be "of great and permanent benefit to this community."[165]

In 1925, a new building was constructed on the same location, and on April 25, 1927, the library was re-opened to the public. The library was officially renamed in honour of George A. Saden, a retired Superior Court Judge who died in 2003. Now spanning five locations, the central branch of the library is known as the Burroughs and Saden Memorial Library.[166]

The Bridgeport Libraries' mission includes a statement on how libraries can change people's lives and provides opportunities for area residents to "pursue lifelong learning, cultural and economic enrichment and enjoyment."[167]

THE GHOST OF DOCTOR HARRIS

The Boston Athenaeum Library

Boston, Massachusetts

A famous American writer claims to have spied a ghost reading in a Boston library, and was so inspired by his visions that he wrote a now-classic story about it.

Founded in 1807, the Boston Athenaeum is one of the oldest and most distinguished independent libraries in the United States and one of a few membership-based libraries still in existence, relying on patrons paying an annual subscription fee for access to their services.

An athenaeum, by definition, is a building filled with printed material provided for use, or an association of persons interested in scientific or literary pursuits. So, just as a museum might be considered a place for the muses, who inspire art, an athenaeum is a place for Athena, the goddess of wisdom, who inspires intellectual pursuits.

Famous American writer Nathaniel Hawthorne reported that he spied the ghost of Reverend Thaddeus Mason Harris reading the *Boston Post* in one particular chair in the Athenaeum's reading room, and that he continued to see the man's ghost in the same seat every day that he returned. Hawthorne seemed to be the only person in the reading room who could see the ghost of Harris, and the two had an unspoken relationship as they observed one another in quiet.

Inspired by this experience, Hawthorne wrote a story entitled "The Ghost of Doctor Harris" which was published in chapbook form by Tucker Publishing Co. in 1900.

The full text of Hawthorne's story appears below.

The Athenaeum Centenary (Charles Knowles Bolton), 1907

The Boston Athenaeum Reading Room.

The Ghost of Dr. Harris by Nathaniel Hawthorne[168]

I am afraid this ghost story will be a very faded aspect when transferred to paper. Whatever effect is had on you, or whatever charm it retains in your memory, is perhaps to be attributed to the favourable circumstances under which it was originally told.

We were sitting, I remember, late in the evening, in your drawing-room, where the lights of the chandelier were so muffled as to produce a delicious obscurity through which the fire diffused a dim red glow. In this rich twilight the feelings of the party had been properly attuned by some tales of English superstition, and the lady of Smithills Hall had just been describing that Bloody Footstep which marks the threshold of her old mansion, when your Yankee guest (zealous for the honour of his country, and desirous of proving that his dead compatriots have the same ghostly privileges as other dead people, if they think it worthwhile to use them) began a story of something wonderful that long ago happened to himself. Possibly in the verbal narrative he may have assumed a little more licence than would be allowable in a written record. For the sake of the artistic effect, he may then have thrown in, here and there, a few slight circumstances which he will not think it proper to retain in what he now puts forth as the sober statement of a veritable fact.

A good many years ago (it must be as many as fifteen, perhaps more, and while I was still a bachelor) I resided at Boston, in the United States. In that city there is a large and long-established library, styled the Athenaeum, connected with which is a reading-room, well supplied with foreign and American periodicals and newspapers. A splendid edifice has since been erected by the proprietors of the institution; but, at the period I speak of, it was contained within a large old mansion, formerly the town residence of an eminent citizen of Boston. The reading-room (a spacious hall, with the group of the Laocoon at one end, and the Belvedere Apollo at the other) was frequented by not a few elderly merchants, retired from business, by clergymen and lawyers, and by such literary men as we had amongst us. These good people were mostly old, leisurely, and somnolent, and used to nod and doze for hours together, with the newspapers before them (ever and anon recovering themselves as far as to read a word or two of the politics of the day) sitting, as, as it were, on the boundary of the Land of Dreams, and having little to do with this world, except through the newspapers which they so tenaciously grasped.

One of these worthies, whom I occasionally saw there, was the Reverend Doctor Harris, a Unitarian clergyman of considerable repute and eminence. He was very far advanced in life, not less than eighty years old, and probably more; and he resided, I think, at Dorchester, a suburban village in the immediate vicinity of Boston. I had never been personally acquainted with this good old clergyman, but had heard of him all my life as a noteworthy man; so that when he was first pointed out to me I looked at him with a certain specialty of attention, and always subsequently eyed him with a degree of interest whenever I happened to see him at the Athenaeum or elsewhere. He was a small, withered, infirm, but brisk old gentleman, with snow-white hair, a somewhat stooping figure, but yet a remarkable alacrity of movement. I remember it was in the street that I first noticed him. The Doctor was plodding along with a staff, but turned smartly about on being addressed by the gentleman who was with me, and responded with a good deal of vivacity.

"Who is he?" I inquired, as soon as he had passed.

"The Reverend Doctor Harris, of Dorchester," replied my companion; and from that time I often saw him, and never forgot his aspect. His especial haunt was the Athenaeum. There I used to see him daily, and almost always with a newspaper 'the Boston Post,' which was the leading journal of the Democratic Party in the Northern States. As old doctor Harris had been a noted Democrat during his more active life, it was a very natural thing, it was a very natural thing that he should still like to read the Boston Post. There his reverend figure was accustomed to sit day after day, in the self-same chair by the fireside; and, by degrees, seeing him there so constantly, I began to look toward him as I entered the reading-room, and felt that a kind of acquaintance, at least on my part, was established. Not that I had any reason (as long as this venerable person remained in the body) to suppose that he ever noticed me; but by some subtle connection, that small, white-haired, infirm, yet vivacious figure of an old clergyman became associated with my idea

and recollection of the place. One day especially (about noon, as was generally his hour) I
am perfectly certain that I had seen this figure
of old Doctor Harris, and taken my customary
note of him, although I remember nothing in
his appearance at all different from what I had
seen on many previous occasions.

But, that very evening, a friend said to me:
"Did you hear that old Doctor Harris is dead?"

"No," said I very quietly, "and it cannot be
true; for I saw him at the Athenaeum to-day."

"You must be mistaken," rejoined my friend.
"He is certainly dead!" and confirmed the fact
with such special circumstances that I could no
longer doubt it. My friend has often since assured
me that I seemed much startled as the intelli-
gence; but, as well as I can recollect, I believe that
I was very little disturbed, if at all, but set down
the apparition as a mistake of my own, or, perhaps, the interposition of a familiar idea into the
place and amid the circumstances with which I
had been accustomed to associate it.

The next day, as I ascended the steps of
the Athenaeum, I remember thinking within
myself: "Well, I never shall see old Doctor
Harris again!" With this thought in my mind,
as I opened the door of the reading-room, I
glanced toward the spot and chair where Doctor
Harris usually sat, and there, to my astonish-
ment, sat the grey, infirm figure of the deceased
Doctor, reading the newspaper as was his wont!
His own death must have been recorded, that
very morning, in that very newspaper! I have

no recollection of being greatly discomposed at the moment, or indeed that I felt any extraordinary emotion whatever. Probably, if ghosts were in the habit of coming among us, they would coincide with the ordinary train of affairs, and melt into them so familiarly that we should not be shocked at their presence. At all events, so it was in this instance. I looked through the newspapers as usual, and turned over the periodicals, taking about as much interest in their contents as at other times. Once or twice, no doubt, I may have lifted my eyes from the page to look again at the venerable Doctor, who ought then to have been lying in his coffin dressed out for the grave, but who felt such interest in the Boston Post as to come back from the other world to read it the morning after his death. One might have supposed that he would have cared more about the novelties of the sphere to which he had just been introduced than about the politics he had left behind him! The apparition took no notice of me, nor behaved otherwise in any respect than on any previous day. Nobody but myself seemed to notice him, and yet the old gentlemen round about the fire, beside his chair, were his lifelong acquaintances, who were perhaps thinking of his death, and who in a day or two would deem it a proper courtesy to attend his funeral.

I have forgotten how the ghost of Doctor Harris took its departure from the Athenaeum on this occasion, or, in fact, whether the ghost or I went first. This equanimity, and almost indifference, on my part (the careless way in which I glanced at so singular a mystery and left it aside) is what now surprises me as much as anything else in the affair.

From that time, for a long time thereafter (for weeks at least, and I know not but for months) I used to see the figure of Doctor Harris quite as frequently as before his death. It grew to be so common that at length I regarded the venerable defunct no more than any other of the old fogies who basked before the fire and dozed over the newspapers.

It was but a ghost (nothing but thin air) not tangible nor appreciable, nor demanding any attention from a man of flesh and blood! I cannot recollect any cold shudderings, any awe, any repugnance, any emotion whatever, such as would be suitable and decorous on beholding a visitant from the spiritual world. It is very strange, but such is the truth. It appears excessively odd to me now that I did not adopt such means as I readily might to ascertain whether the appearance had solid substance, or was merely gaseous and vapoury. I might have brushed against him, have jostled his chair or have trodden accidentally on his poor old toes. I might have snatched the Boston Post (unless that were an apparition, too) out of his shadowy hands. I might have tested him in a hundred ways; but I did nothing of the kind.

Perhaps I was loath to destroy the illusion, and to rob myself of so good a ghost story, which might probably have been explained in some very commonplace way. Perhaps, after all,

I had a secret dread of the old phenomenon, and therefore kept within my limits, with an instinctive caution which I mistook for indifference. Be this as it may, here is the fact. I saw the figure, day after day, for a considerable space of time, and took no pains to ascertain whether it was a ghost or no. I never, to my knowledge, saw him come into the reading-room or depart from it. There sat Doctor Harris in his customary chair, and I can say little else about him.

After a certain period (I really know not how long) I began to notice, or to fancy, a peculiar regard in the old gentleman's aspect toward myself. I sometimes found him gazing at me, and, unless I deceived myself, there was a sort of expectancy in his face. His spectacles, I think, were shoved up, so that his bleared eyes might meet my own. Had he been a living man I should have flattered myself that good Doctor Harris was, for some reason or other, interested in me and desirous of a personal acquaintance. Being a ghost, and amenable to ghostly laws, it was natural to conclude that he was waiting to be spoken to before delivering whatever message he wished to impart. But, if so, the ghost had shown the bad judgement common among the spiritual brotherhood, both as regarded the place of interview and the person whom he had selected as the recipient of his communications. In the reading-room of the Athenaeum conversation is strictly forbidden, and I could not have addressed the apparition without drawing the instant notice and indignant frowns of the

slumberous old gentlemen around me. I myself,
too, at that time, was shy as any ghost, and followed the ghosts' rule never to speak first. And
what an absurd figure should I have made, sol-
emnly and awfully addressing what must have
appeared, in the eyes of all the rest of the company, an empty chair! Besides, I had never been
introduced to Doctor Harris, dead or alive, and
I am not aware that social regulations are to be
abrogated by the accidental fact of one of the
parties having crossed the imperceptible line
which separates the other party from the spiritual world. If ghosts throw off all convention-
alism among themselves, it does not therefore
follow that it can be safely dispensed with by
those who are still hampered with flesh and
blood.

For such reasons as these (and reflecting,
moreover, that the deceased Doctor might
burden me with some disagreeable task, with
which I had no business nor wish to be concerned) I stubbornly resolved to have nothing
to say to him. To this determination I adhered;
and not a syllable ever passed between the ghost
of Doctor Harris and myself.

To the best of my recollection, I never
observed the old gentleman either enter the
reading-room or depart from it, or move from
his chair, or lay down the newspaper, or exchange
a look with any person in the company, unless it
sere myself. He was not by any means invariably
in his place. In the evening, for instance, though
often at the reading-room myself, I never saw

him. It was at the brightest noontide that I used to behold him, sitting within the most comfortable focus of the glowing fire, as real and lifelike an object (except that he was so very old, and of an ashen complexion) as any other in the room. After a long while of this strange intercourse, if such it can be called, I remember (once at least, and I know not but oftener) a sad, wistful, disappointed gaze, which the ghost fixed upon me from beneath his spectacles; a melancholy look of helplessness, which, if my heart had not been as hard as a paving-stone, I could hardly have withstood. But I did withstand it; and I think I saw him no more after this last appealing look, which still dwells in my memory as perfectly as while my own eyes were encountering the dim and bleared eyes of the ghost. And whenever I recall this strange passage of my life, I see the small, old withered figure of Dr. Harris, sitting in his accustomed chair, the Boston Post in his hand, his spectacles shoved upwards and gazing at me as I close the door of the reading-room, with that wistful, appealing, hopeless, helpless look. It is too late now: his grave has been grass-grown this many and many a year; and I hope he has found rest in it without any aid from me.

I have only to add that it was not until long after I had ceased to encounter the ghost that I became aware how very odd and strange the whole affair had been; and even now I am made sensible of its strangeness chiefly by the wonder and incredulity of those to whom I tell the story.

As Hawthorne describes, his encounter with Doctor Harris was indeed an "odd and strange" affair, one that he was loathe to destroy the illusion of by trying to, for example, snap the newspaper away from the spectre before him.

Hawthorne isn't of course, the only person to have witnessed something truly bizarre and strange in this particular Boston location. As you'll see in a later chapter in this book (When A Book Gets Under Your Skin), stranger things than well-read ghosts reside among the stacks of this literary locale.

WHEN I DIE, I'LL LEAVE YOU MY BOOKS AND MY GHOST

Charleston Library Society

Charleston, South Carolina

One of the oldest libraries in the United States, housing a wealth of special collections, the Charleston Library Society also houses a kindred spirit. This ghost might have left more than a significant collection to the library; he also bequeathed his own spirit.[169]

William Godber Hinson was a nineteenth-century planter, soldier, and book collector. When Hinson died in 1919, he bequeathed a significant collection to the Library Society. Because of various unexplainable occurrences and eyewitness accounts over the years, some say that Hinson has returned, after his death, to stay close to the beloved books and papers that he collected throughout his life.[170]

Catherine Slater, one of the former heads of the library, reported that she had seen the spectral image of a man with a full beard dressed in a top hat, nice suit, and heavy clothes. A similar description has been given by other people when relaying their interaction with the ghost.[171]

Library staff quip that the ghost of W.G. Hinson is playful and a bit mischievous, toying with the microfilm machines — perhaps because they are something not from his world, an intriguing technology for the ghost to explore. Similarly, the elevator has been known to operate completely on its own, sometimes running all night despite nobody being inside to operate it. Could this be Hinson's ghost exploring yet another technological marvel?[172]

Reference librarian Carol Jones admitted that the library, or the building itself, definitely has some sort of presence inside of it.[173]

"It gives me the chills," Jones was quoted as saying in a 2007 *Post and Courier* article. "If you have ever been here at night, with the lights out, you know it's just creepy."[174]

Jones referred to the times that college interns have been sent down to the periodical storage room in order to file magazines, only to rush back with complaints of feeling an odd, cold chill down their neck.

Another time, an intern working alone in the basement reported hearing the sound of books being pulled out from the shelves, then being slipped back in, the friction of their cloth covers making an unmistakable sound. When the intern turned the corner to investigate where the sound was coming from, wondering which other intern or librarian might be there, they were shocked to discover they were alone in the basement. That intern shot out of the building and refused to return to the library afterward.

In a 2007 article from the *Post and Courier*, journalist Brian Hicks interviewed assistant librarian Janice Knight, who caught a glimpse of a man she identified as Hinson as she was stepping through the doorway of the library one morning. He was not spectral at all, however, but entirely solid. He was standing at the far end of the table, and she saw him there for at least a few seconds before he completely disappeared. He didn't fade out — he suddenly vanished.[175]

"It [his clothing] was not something anyone wears anymore," Knight said in the interview. "And it wasn't something from my father's time."[176]

Staff have also reported that certain portraits, perhaps even one of Hinson that hangs in the main reading room, have leapt off the walls and fallen to the floor all on their own. Several of the no-nonsense librarians attribute this phenomenon to vibrations caused by delivery trucks rumbling by on the street just outside the building, but others wonder if it might be Hinson doing a bit of afterlife redecoration.

A group of seventeen men of various trades and professions established the Charleston Library Society in December of 1748, making it one of the country's oldest libraries. This pioneering movement led to the founding of the College of Charleston in 1770 and also provided the core collection for natural history artifacts for the 1773 Charleston Museum.[177]

Among the notable collections contained in this library are Colonial era newspapers, rare fifteenth-century manuscripts, letters autographed by George Washington, and John Locke's *The Fundamental Constitutions of the Carolinas.*

THE CURSE OF OLD LADY GRAY

Peoria Public Library

Peoria, Illinois

The land that the Peoria Public Library was built on was cursed more than 175 years ago. However, the first reported casualty of the curse did not take place for 150 years; but that death, and a few others that occurred in the following decade, have helped escalate the stories about the "The Curse of Old Lady Gray."

In the 1830s, Andrew and Mary Gray lived in a two-storey home on North Monroe Street. Local legend has it that Mary Stevenson Gray was an enthusiastic gardener and enjoyed spending time cultivating the land their home stood on. When Mary's brother died and her drunken, lazy, and troublesome nephew came to live with the elderly couple, he became an ongoing concern — and caused much grief for Mary.[178]

As time passed, Mary's nephew's reputation for socializing with disreputable characters, as well as his immoral and drunken behaviour, resulted in an ongoing acquaintance with the local authorities. Mary and her husband ended up incurring significant expenses for lawyer fees asssociated with defending her nephew in court. The debt accrued to local lawyer David Davis was so high that Andrew and Mary had to use the mortgage on the Gray property in order to secure the attorney fees.[179]

Demanding his unpaid fees, Davis eventually brought a lawsuit against the Grays to foreclose on the mortgage. Angry and at her wit's end, Mary turned her drunken nephew out of her home. He spent the rest of his days drunk, angry, and bewildered, living on the streets and then eventually disappearing. His bloated corpse was discovered some time later, floating in the Illinois River.[180]

Devastated with the final blow against her home and her family, Mary Gray, in a fit of anger and grief, cursed the very ground her home stood on with "thorns and thistles, ill luck, sickness and death to its every owner and occupant."[181]

As legend has it, the curse took effect almost immediately.

No sooner had the legal action removed ownership of the property from the Grays than the once rich and fertile soil began to sprout nothing but spindly weeds. Maintenance workers refused to work on the allegedly cursed land and the once beautifully manicured and cultivated grounds became an overgrown eyesore, and the building itself became decrepit. The deserted property was overrun with rats, and people shared stories about hearing the ghost of Mary's nephew crying for forgiveness at the home's front door, begging to be let in.[182, 183]

Davis, the lawyer, also seemed to suffer an ill side-effect of his action against the Gray property. Despite his previous prestige in the community, his actions in regards to the Gray family led to village folks shunning him and his business. Davis never recaptured his previous popularity as a lawyer, never did take ownership of the Gray property, and eventually moved his practice to nearby Bloomington.[184]

Deserted and left overgrown, the old Gray home sat undisturbed and vacant until one winter night, when it inexplicably burst into flames. Legend has it that local villagers claimed to have seen the ghost of Old Lady Gray appear in the flames, laughing and dancing with delight at the home's destruction.[185]

Over time the property, which locals would cross the street to avoid walking alongside for fear of the alleged curse on the grounds, was sold off to pay the property taxes. A new home was built on the land, with rooms available for rent.[186]

The next family to move into a home on that property was that of ex-governor Thomas Ford, who had already had a curse thrown onto his home and family by Mormon leader Joseph Smith after Ford raised taxes and sent soldiers to Nauvoo in order to end a bout of guerilla warfare. Some believe that the intersection of the Ford Curse and the Gray Curse might have been the cause of the intense devastation that wracked his life and family.[187]

Shortly after his wife died in October 1850, Ford died in deep debt, described as an old, feeble, broken, and forgotten man in his final years. All three of his daughters died of consumption in a relatively short period of time, and his son, Tom, was killed in an incident where he had been mistaken for a cattle rustler.[188]

The Ford home was eventually torn down and the next person to move onto the land was an ex-slave by the name of Tom Lindsay. Lindsay had recently been freed by the Emancipation Proclamation, and the son of his ex-master purchased a portion of the property and allowed him to live there. Lindsay erected a small shack, which was struck by lightning and burned to the ground. After learning about the curse, when Lindsay rebuilt a home, he buried a petrified rabbit's foot under the front entrance and hung horseshoes in every room of the house.[189] The man's superstitious ritual seemed to have done the trick for him, because Lindsay lived in the home undisturbed by the "Gray Curse" for a quarter of a century.[190]

However, in the decades following Lindsay's departure, several more residents of the property suffered a series of eerie fates. The first was a local businessman whose wife died tragically within the first year of the couple obtaining ownership of the property. The next was a banker whose wife died shortly after giving birth to a baby boy; the child died soon after. That same banker remarried and he and his new wife also had a boy. That boy, who suffered a bizarre affliction wherein he avoided warmth, was often found sleeping in the cold front hallway of the home in the depths of winter. He too, died. His mother's grief and despair was so deep that she was sent off to Minneapolis in an attempt to recover her sanity. The next resident of the cursed site was a boarding room housekeeper whose son plunged to his death from a hot-air balloon, and whose daughter drowned in the nearby river.[191]

In October 1855, Peoria Library Services began by opening not one, but two separate locations.[192] The continued growth eventually bisected with the cursed land, when in June 1894 three lots on Northeast Monroe Street were purchased by the City of Peoria.[193]

E.S. Willcox, who had been responsible for initiating the state law provisions permitting the establishment of public libraries, was appointed head librarian in February 1891.[194, 195]

Twenty years later, on April 6, 1915, Mr. Willcox was heading home from the library when he suffered an unfortunate accident crossing the street. While crossing the busy road, Willcox failed to notice an approaching streetcar and stepped directly in front of it. Despite the streetcar operator's sounding of the gong and attempts to stop the vehicle, Mr. Willcox was struck by the fender, suffered a deep gash to the head, and was taken, unconscious, to the local Proctor Hospital where he was officially pronounced dead.[196, 197]

Erastus S. Willcox's successor, S. Patterson Prowse, died in the library on December 14, 1921 from a heart attack, under curious circumstances. During a late-afternoon board meeting, Prowse, who had been showing no signs of illness, engaged in a lively and spirited debate. As the meeting adjourned, Prowse got up to leave the boardroom and suddenly collapsed, unconscious, to the floor. A nearby doctor summoned to the scene was unable to resuscitate the man, speculating that he might very well have been dead before he even hit the ground.[198]

Dr. Edwin Wiley, the next librarian, accepted his position in the spring of 1922. Interested in performing positive community service, Wiley was responsible for creating the Bedside Book Service, a program where books were brought to the bedsides of the invalid and infirm of area hospitals. He also established the "Open Book" policy, whereby the public could access books directly rather than requiring library staff to retrieve the books for them.[199]

In the early morning of October 20, 1924, Dr. Wiley's wife woke to the sound of her husband groaning in pain. When she inquired about his discomfort, he told her that he had ingested arsenic. A physician was called and attempts were made to pump the poison from Wiley's stomach. The man remained conscious for most of the efforts andwas able to speak. He did not, however, offer any explanation as to why he would have swallowed the arsenic found in a collection of chemicals that his son (a student at Bradley Polytechnic Institute) kept stored in their house. Despite attempts to purge the poison from Wiley's system, he died from arsenic poisoning.[200]

Though there were three consecutive librarian deaths, all occurring within a relatively short time period in the library's history, no additional librarians seem to have suffered from any sort of similar curse. Odd and eerie occurrences, however, continued to be reported in the library.

Strange gusts of cold air with no detectable origin, the sound of books toppling to the floor heard in places where not a single tome was out of place, doors opening and closing of their own volition, and apparitions appearing in library mirrors have all been reported over the years.[201]

John B. Kachuba, author of *Ghosthunting Illinois*, describes standing in a particular spot just outside a set of elevator doors and feeling intense cold, and a sense that he was floating, his feet slowly being lifted off the floor, and a dizzy light-headedness. The feeling left him the moment he stepped away from the spot. A library staff member accompanying Kachuba explained to him that everybody felt the same thing when standing on that spot, but nobody knew what caused it.[202]

Kachuba, in conversations with librarian staff, learned that some staff reported a ghostly wailing, as if someone might be in pain, lights flickering on and off on their own, and even a staff member's chair shooting about three feet across the floor.[203]

A custodian reported seeing an elderly man, nicely attired in black garb, wandering the library. When she followed him to see if he was lost and needed help finding something, she was surprised to find him vanish around the corner of a set of shelves. The woman insisted that the man was similar in description to original head librarian E.S. Willcox.[204]

Others also reported seeing a man dressed in turn-of-the-century clothing disappearing around the corner of the stacks or moving through one of the aisles. One theory is that this apparition is, like the custodian suggests, the spirit of one of the library's cursed founding fathers continuing on in his eternal support of the library's goals.[205]

WHEN A GHOST CALLS YOUR NAME

Brand Library
Glendale, California

It's not often that a ghost calls you by name. But when it does — like one did to Joseph Fuchs — you'd better pay heed.

The Brand Library resides in a former mansion built by Leslie Coombs Brand in 1904. Brand died in the building in 1925, and, according to popular stories, haunts the former home that he bequeathed to the city, uttering single word cries, descending the stairs, or asserting his presence in various locations.[206]

In an article entitled "Something Ghostly This Way Comes" written by Nancy Garza in a 1993 article from *Glendale News Press*, Library Services Administrator Joseph Fuchs reported something odd that happened to him when he was alone in the library one dark and moonless night.[207]

In the process of packing up his things to leave for the evening, at around 8:00 p.m., Fuchs paused in the doorway of his

Portrait of Leslie Brand.

office, taking a quick moment to ensure that he had packed every-thing he needed in his satchel.[208]

That's when he heard the low moan of a voice speak to him: "Joe!"[209]

Fuchs spun around, surprised there was someone else still there. But when he looked, he was all alone.[210] Fuchs glared at the centre of the stairwell, where he had detected the voice, but nobody was there.[211]

That's when the realization of what he had heard began to sink in.[212] He originally thought that he had heard someone call out his name, "Joe!" A chill settled on his spine when he realized that the ghastly deep moan had uttered the command, "Go!"[213]

He beat a hasty retreat down the staircase, making sure to turn on all of the lights in succession as he fled the building.[214]

Another time, Fuchs had been working in a room at the bottom of the stairs, carrying a pile of books to a nearby table, when he spotted a male figure climbing the stairs toward a floor that was off limits to the public. When he turned his head, ready to call out to the stranger, the image vanished before his eyes.[215]

Other witnesses report feeling their hair stand on end for no reason when entering certain parts of the building, hearing foot-steps coming from a vacant room overhead, shadows flitting about on the staircase, and books suddenly falling over all on their own.[216]

A tower in the mansion continues to be a location that staff members refuse to work in alone. "There seemed to be a feeling of a presence," Fuchs said. "And there was a cold air that all of a sudden would come out of nowhere."

Custodial staff also refuse to work alone in particular locations in the library, and investigative ghost hunters are convinced that the eerie spectral visions and overwhelming feeling of a cold presence in the building must be that of Brand.

Outside the library lies the Brand Family Cemetery, where a large mausoleum stands along additional graves and a stone marker. Brand and several of his family members are supposedly laid to rest in that location. Apart from the remote location being a popular make-out spot for teenagers, there are stories about a baby buried in that location that can be heard crying on cold, dark nights.[217]

Considering the effort that Brand made to make the home so spectacular, could it simply be that the man could not leave it, even after he died?

The Brand Library and Art Center is located in the foothills overlooking Glendale and the San Fernando Valley. It is housed in the former mansion built by Leslie Coombs Brand in 1904. Named El Miradero, the architecture was inspired by the East Indian Pavilion that had been built for the 1893 World's Columbian Exposition held in Chicago. Consisting of five bedrooms, a parlour, drawing room, living room, dining room, music salon, and solarium, the interior of the home was richly decorated with Tiffany leaded-glass windows, handcrafted woodwork, and silk damask wall coverings.[218,219]

The Brand Library opened in 1956. The building and land were bequeathed by Brand to the city with a provision that the property be used specifically for a library and a public park. Various renovations over the years have ensured that the Brand Library and Art Center, which includes a library, a park, an art gallery, and a recital hall, are a vibrant and central cultural hub for the local community.[220]

NOT SO SWEET WHEN YOU BUILD ON A GRAVE

Sweetwater County Library

Green River, Wyoming

Despite the bodies and grave markers being moved from the North 1st East Street locale before any building took place in 1926, buried bodies keep being unearthed on the grounds where Sweetwater County Library now stands; but if that weren't creepy enough, the staff report odd supernatural occurrences inside, from unexplained noises and smells to sightings of spirits wandering among the shelves.[221, 222]

Eerie and unexplainable occurrences happen so often, in fact, that in 1993 the staff launched a "Ghost Log" in which these odd experiences could be recorded and shared.[223]

The Ghost Log, which is replicated on a website called *High Spirits: The Ghost Log Blog*, contains well over a hundred entries of eerie experiences recorded between 1993 and 2008. Instances include voices, lights switching on and off on their own, smells as diverse as strong perfume to the odour of fish, tapping in adjacent vacant bathroom stalls, and snippets of music.[224]

"Most people are curious," librarian Micki Gilmore said in a 2011 interview with *The Green River Star*. "We don't have all the answers, we just know that people are curious."[225]

Gilmore, who says the staff have alternatively referred to the library's ghosts as either "Caspar the Friendly Ghost" or "Moaning Myrtle," also points out that despite instances of people being creeped out and frightened by what they have seen and heard, nothing evil or bad has ever occurred in the library as a result of the alleged haunting.[226]

But back to the bodies.

An old city cemetery was located at the very same spot where the library was built. The cemetery was in use from the 1870s until 1913. In 1926, the bodies and all of the markers were moved to a new cemetery location, and about fifteen years later a series of homes for returning World War II veterans was built there. When they were no longer needed, the homes were removed and the lot stood vacant until construction of the new library began in 1978.[227]

Architect Neil Stowe was walking the site behind a Caterpillar that was moving through and loosening the soil, when he spotted what looked like a deteriorated coconut sitting in the freshly churned dirt. He picked it up, turned it around, and immediately recognized it as part of a skull. "Little tufts of brown hair were still clinging to it," he said.[228]

Stowe reported that somewhere between eight and ten more bodies were discovered in unmarked graves.[229]

A few years later, while working on some landscaping for the site, contractors uncovered some buried planks of wood in front of the main doors to the library. At first they thought it might be old buried construction debris that had resurfaced, at least until they spotted the bones.[230]

The coroner was called in and they started pulling the bodies out until they ran into a problem. A few of the skeletons were caught underneath the sidewalk and couldn't be removed without first tearing out the concrete. They ended up taking out only whatever body parts they could. "First they dug out three adults — actually I should say two and a half," Ed Johnson, a maintenance man who had worked in the building at the time said, "because on one body they just pulled out the legs and pelvic girdle and left the rest. They also found one infant grave, and I believe they were able to take only the foot and shin bones from it."[231]

In 1985, further structural work was required on the building. "The building had begun to sink," Johnson said. "While the construction workers were drilling into the foundation, one said that they found a whole, small coffin with the body of another child inside. This corpse was almost perfectly preserved. The flesh was like gelatin, but otherwise, everything was intact."[232]

The 1990s construction on the street adjacent to the library uncovered the remains of a man and a woman who had been in their forties when they died.[233]

Johnson reported constantly having the feeling of being watched. And on one particular occasion, when he was vacuuming back and forth between the stacks, he ended up moving too far and inadvertently pulling the plug. "Naturally, the vacuum quit working," he said, "so I turned the switch off and went back down the stacks to plug in the fifty-foot cord."[234]

But before he could walk all the way back to turn the vacuum on again, it started up all on its own. Johnson then unplugged the vacuum again, wound up the cord and said to whatever unseen presence was there, "Okay guys, the building's yours. I'm going home!"[235]

Another staff member reports vacuuming in the multi-purpose room when she glanced up at an adjoining stage. The curtains were open and the stage was set up for a forthcoming event. She remembered thinking how nice it all looked and went back to her cleaning. When she looked back up a few minutes later, the curtains were closed.[236]

Don Leasor, another maintenance man, was also vacuuming when something odd happened to him. While running the vacuum he heard the distinct rattling of what sounded like a keyring. "Whatever was making the noise was in the same room with me," he said. "And whenever I'd shut the vacuum off, the noise would stop, too."[237]

Leasor, who had worked in the building since 1986, also spotted mysterious glowing lights inside the building one night when he had been ready to walk out the door. When he turned off the lights, he saw small glowing lights moving over the wall above the entranceway, as if somebody inside was shining pen-light flashlights. The glowing appeared and disappeared every three to four seconds.[238]

Another time Leasor heard strains of what sounded like Beethoven coming from the multi-purpose room, despite there being nobody in the room, and in what he describes as his most frightening experience, he heard ghostly voices coming from that same room.[239]

"It sounded like a man and a woman yelling and arguing," he said, explaining that he had just returned from taking out the trash, believing himself to be the only one in the building at the time. "Although the words were muffled so I couldn't tell what they were saying." Checking to make sure the voices weren't coming from outside, Leasor finally steeled himself enough nerve to open the doors to the multi-purpose room. "As soon as I did, the voices immediately stopped!"[240]

Another former staff member was so shaken with the experience of hearing voices that he was too terrified to be interviewed by author Debra Munn when she was writing about the library.[241]

Other staff reported lights turning on and off by themselves in the multi-purpose room and two staff witnessed the wheelchair wrought iron bypass for the security gate slam open as if from a forceful push, then oscillate back and forth for several seconds before closing entirely on its own.[242]

Library director Helen Higby, concerned with so much odd phenomenon occurring after dark, rearranged staff schedules to make sure nobody ever worked alone at night.[243]

"Whatever is going on," Higby said, "if it's some kind of being, apparently it's benign, because it hasn't done anything destructive or harmful. And in a library, you could make a big mess in a hurry if you wanted to by throwing the books on the floor or dumping the card catalogue."[244]

THE DEDICATED GHOST OF IDA DAY

Hutchinson Public Library

Hutchinson, Kansas

When she was living, Ida Day Holzapfel was described as being a librarian twenty-four hours a day. After she died, it seems she kept up with her unworldly commitment to the Hutchinson Public Library.

Ida, who served twice as head librarian, was described as totally dedicated by her former secretary, Eunice Pankow, in a 1975 *Hutchinson News* article. Pankow went on to state that, though her boss's dedication sometimes gave other employees the impression that she might be difficult to work with — particularly because there was no way that other employees could possibly live up to her tireless dedication — Ida was probably the best librarian she had ever been privileged to work with in her twenty-four-year career at the library.[245]

Though Ida loved the library and enjoyed the ritual, she eventually desired an escape from her administrative duties, and tendered her resignation in 1954 to accept a position as reference librarian for Tulare County in California.[246] She never had a chance to realize the new role, as she reportedly died in an automobile accident on the first day of her new job.[247]

Around the time of Ida's death, Angeline Welch, a reference librarian at the time, began reporting that she was experiencing the presence "of someone who had worked in the library before" when she was in the basement.[248]

Library employee Rose Hale was returning to the basement when she heard Welch, who was downstairs shelving books, speaking with someone. She arrived at the bottom of the stairs and heard the echo of retreating footsteps. She then asked Welch with whom she had been speaking, Welch responded by saying she hadn't been speaking with anyone.

It was only the next day over lunch that Welch admitted to speaking with a lady she had never seen before, who had been standing at the bottom of the stairs. The stranger had asked Welch what she was doing, and just as Welch had started to explain the task she was engaged in, Hale had begun to descend the stairs. That was when the inquisitive woman began walking away to some unknown location in the basement.[249] As Welch began to describe the lady in detail, Hale realized that Welch, who had never met Ida, was describing the former librarian in detail. Welch insisted that the woman she had met had not been a spirit, but a physical human.[250]

After that time, employees continued to report hearing the sound of footsteps echoing in the basement, although only one of them, Dorothy Oyler, claimed to actually believe in ghosts. "I had no doubts," Oyler told reporter Judy Williams. "I believe in these types of things. But it has to be a person who is deeply motivated."[251]

Hutchinson News

k look and she said 'nothing.' And ut who were you talking to and she ody'—but I could hear the footving. I didn't see anything and I l anything."

Ida Day returns?
dale said Ms. Welch told her the that where she stopped below the lady was standing, but she didn't o the lady was. That day the two nd Dorothy Oyler went to lunch laAfter Angeline described the who she saw in the basement the re, Mrs. Oyler, who had worked , Holzapfei exclaimed, "Well then scribing Ida Day."
was the first time Ms. Welch had rd of the former librarian, accordrs. Hale. Mrs. Hale said the figure oman in the basement asked Mrs. hat she was doing, and then the figied away because she could hear teps—but to where it walked she ow,
that time, some employes said they rd footsteps in the basement.
time Ms. Welch said she saw in the basement, that was not in a m but in human form, the public upposed to be in the basement benew addition to the library was struction and employes were work

Extra sense
ne Welch was described by her ere as one who possesses some sort sense that makes her highly atd sensitive to those around her. ne person interviewed, who talked ghost story, said she actually beghosts, Dorothy Oyler said she has lar experiences, but none with Ida t all those interviewed believed ch was 100 per cent serious in exher experience with the former liAnd most thought she had seen Mrs. Holzapfel.

"I had no doubts," said Mrs. Oyler. "I believe in these type of things. But it has to be a person who is deeply motivated."
"If she wanted to haunt any place, it would probably be here," said Mrs. Black. "She might be concerned with they way things are going on here sometimes."

No joke
Ruth Sanders, who had worked with Mrs. Holzapfel and is now head of the rotating book truck for South Central Kansas library system, said she didn't view the story as a joke. "I know different people have different experiences and just because I haven't had any doesn't mean that others don't." Several other of the women expressed similar views.
Some of the younger employes, according to Mrs. Gordon, don't like to go down to the basement alone. "When it's dark and someone has to go down to the basement then every sound they hear, they think it's Ida Day. After night when it's all dark, I don't like to step down there either, but I'm not concerned about Ida Day."
It has also become an office joke that whenever anything at the library is misplaced or missing, they blame it on Ida Day.
The feeling, both seriously with some and lightly with others, is that Ida Day Holzapfel has returned to watch over the library and sometimes rebels when she doesn't think it is being run right.
But who's to decide? In a story published in The Hutchinson News about Mrs. Holzapfel resigning to take a new job in California, the article reads, "She plans to retain ownership of her home at 430 East 12th and will eventually return to Hutchinson..."

Footnote—The reporter writing the story attempted to call Angeline Welch several times for her verification of the story, but was unable to reach her. Ms. Welch is reportedly going to law school and is living in Glendale, Calif.

"TALKING OF ghosts . . . it is undecid whether or not there has ever been an instance the spirit of any person appearing after death. All gument is against it, but all belief is for it." —) Samuel Johnson

Article "Does a ghost haunt the library" from *Hutchinson News*, Oct 31, 1975.

Junivee Black, a children's librarian who was a protégé of the former librarian, said, "If she wanted to haunt any place, it would probably be here." She even joked that Ida "might be concerned with the way things are going on here sometimes."[252]

Other staff members took to joking that when something was misplaced or lost that it must be Ida's ghost that was responsible. Some of the younger staff members were uncomfortable with going down to the basement alone, and over time more reports of Ida's full-bodied appearances, as well as odd bangs coming from the basement, were reported in the library.[253, 254]

Considering the dedication to propriety Ida showed during her life, it wouldn't be surprising if, eventually, a patron reports a woman matching Ida's description boldly shushing them for speaking too loudly in the stacks.

At the beginning of the twentieth century, the city of Hutchinson had no public library to speak of. By 1901, the Women's Club had amassed a collection of nearly five hundred volumes, which they wanted to present to the city in order to create a free public library. A Board of Trustees was formed, and with a donation from Andrew Carnegie in the amount of $15,000, the new library was opened on January 19, 1904. Serving the City of Hutchinson and the surrounding towns in Reno County and beyond, the library's mission continues to be about meeting the reading, learning, and information needs of its patrons.[255, 256]

A ROWDY, HIDDEN PRESENCE

Hidden Passage Books

Placerville, California

Over a series of years, Hidden Passage Books's owners reported cool breezes, books falling off shelves, cords being unplugged, and the odd sound of glass tinkling, almost as if some unseen presence was having a dainty tea party somewhere in the bookstore.[257]

Although no longer open, Hidden Passage Books was located in a building that dated back to the mid-1880s, when Placerville, then known as "Dry Diggins," began to develop as a city. The site the store was on housed, at various times, a saloon, a tannery, and three different bookstores.[258]

In 2007, the California Haunts Paranormal Investigation Team investigated the building, bringing in a heavy arsenal of technical equipment, such as infrared cameras, digital voice recorders, electromagnetic field meters, thermometers, and other high tech monitoring devices.[259, 260]

Accompanying psychic Autumn Marr announced, almost the minute she walked into the bookstore, that the name of the spirit there was William.[261]

Before turning off the lights, the research team set up their recording equipment and laid out a sealed bottle of gin and a shot glass. They hoped the props might entice a spirit, which could have been lingering from the time that a saloon had stood on the grounds. In an attempt to appeal to the alleged tinkling of teacups, a saucer and teacup were placed on a shelf.[262]

Once the recording equipment and props were laid out, investigator Ruth Caldwell took dousing rods in hand and started to ask the spirit questions. "I use dousing rods during Electronic Voice Phenomenon sessions," Caldwell said, "because I believe I can allow spirits to control their movement, thus indicating 'yes' or 'no' answers as well as positioning the rods to lead me in a particular direction."[263]

A series of questions lead Caldwell to receive confirmation that there was indeed a spirit present and also that it was male. Throughout the continued interrogation and investigation, the team reported hearing noises emanating from both the back room as well as the attic.[264]

At one point during Caldwell's questioning, she asked the spirit if it could attempt to move the shot glass. The sound of a glass being pushed across a hard surface was audible in the room, but the shot glass they had placed on the table remained perfectly still in front of them. When the team listened to the EVP recording later, they also picked up what sounded like a glass being plunked onto a table just prior to the sound of it dragging across the surface.[265]

Although the investigators didn't pick up much else on their recording devices during that particular investigation, investigator Charlotte Kosa noticed a cold spot that was fifteen degrees cooler than the rest of the room, which seemed to follow her around for the entire evening.[266]

In October 2010, California Haunts psychic Caren Clarke stood outside the building and described a dominant male presence. "On the other side of the wall, there is a strong energy coming through," she said. "A lot of the books, they come pouring down sometimes. My hair is sticking up and I am getting chills. I just keep seeing books falling."[267]

Psychic Nancy Bradley wrote an August 2009 blog post about one of the previous bookstores on the exact same premises. It appears that bookstores by the names of Ravens Tale Books and Rivendell Books were also located in the exact same spot.

Bradley's tale involves a visit she made to the location when owner David Mintz ran the bookstore under the name Rivendell Books. One morning Mintz had heard, just as he was unlocking the door to the store one morning, the sound of people laughing and glasses clinking. However, the moment he stepped inside, the sounds completely disappeared, the store appeared entirely undisturbed, and there was no evidence of anything other than the bookstore he had left the night before.[268]

Shortly after hearing those odd sounds, Mintz started to experience more bizarre phenomenon in the store. Disembodied footsteps could be heard and the smell of stale cigarettes and old clothing permeated the air. Angry voices and aggressive tapping could also be heard and occasionally books would fly off the shelf as if being flung angrily by unseen hands.[269]

Mintz called in Gold Rush Ghosts International Paranormal Investigations, for which Bradley was a psychic investigator. Bradley identified one of the spirits almost immediately as a hangman named Darrell who hanged men on the site of the old Hangman's Tree Bar, located across the street.[270]

Bradley then went on to determine that there were at least a half dozen other spirits active in the building: a couple named Willy and Agnes Grant; a very social character named Samuel Gordan, who referred to himself as "Little Sammy"; a bored woman named Sarah; and an un-named, short, heavy man with a round face and dressed in a dark suit who kept anxiously checking his watch.[271]

The atmosphere in the building appeared rowdy, Bradley explained, as if it was more of a bar or a saloon than a bookstore.[272]

It's no wonder, then, that books were launched from the shelves and onto the floor. It just seems to fit with the many spirits that have lingered on in the building long after the saloon closed down.

MILLICENT THE MUSE

Millicent Library

Fairhaven, Massachusetts

Could the spirit of a girl depicted in a stained-glass window still walk among her beloved books? Millicent Library staff and patrons seem to believe so.

Construction of the library began shortly after the 1890 death of seventeen-year-old Millicent Gifford Rogers, the daughter of library founder Henry Huddleston Rogers, as a tribute to the young girl's love of books and learning.[273] In honour of Millicent, the library features a beautiful stained-glass window bearing her likeness in angelic form, under an image of William Shakespeare and encircled by the names of prominent American writers. Depicted as a muse for great writers, it seems that she also inspired much more recent tales whispered about spirits that walk through the library halls.[274]

Witnesses have claimed they heard Millicent's melodic laughter echoing through the building, or saw her apparition

Carolyn Longworth

Stained glass window featuring Millicent.

strolling through the library surrounded by a brilliant bright-blue aura.[275]

Doreen Skidmore, a librarian who worked at the library since 1989, and Carolyn Longworth, another long-time librarian and current library director, were interviewed for a 2005 article by Rebecca Aubet. Both of the women shared intriguing tales about the library's history and legends. Longworth even took Aubet up to the tower where Millicent is said to look out the window. While poking around the dusty room filled with book-packed shelves, Aubet noted that it might have been the shape of the books as they were visible from the street below that could have made people think that they were seeing a woman through the glass.[276]

Rumours also circulated regarding the possibility that Millicent was buried on the very land where the library stands. However, archivist Debbie Carpentier and library director Carolyn Longworth denied such claims in a 2006 article written for the *Standard-Times*. After that article appeared,

Superintendent of Riverside County Peter Reid confirmed that the girl's remains were in the Rogers family mausoleum.[277] Librarian Doreen Skidmore also quickly dismissed the question with a quick reply: "No, she's buried in the mausoleum with the rest of her family."[278]

Other witnesses claim to have seen a different book-loving woman, dressed entirely in black, walking through the library and running her fingers along the spines of the books.[279] One patron reported an odd occurrence while browsing history books. As he was walking past a row of books, he heard an audible thump from a few feet behind him. He turned and saw one of the books he had just walked past lying on the floor in front of the shelves. He picked the book up and slid it back into its spot on the shelves, and, on his way out, mentioned the odd event to one of the staff at the circulation desk. She shrugged it off, telling him that things like that happened all the time and the staff had simply learned to ignore it.[280]

Still others have reported seeing a man in a tweed jacket with a purple bow tie and tiny, round glasses perched on his nose, mopping the basement floors in spectral form. This same ghost's footfalls have also been heard echoing off the spiral staircase that extends all the way from the library tower down to the basement. Legend says that he is the ghost of a custodian who died, most likely from a heart attack.[281]

Librarian Doreen Skidmore explained to Rebecca Aubet that in the year after the custodian died, there was a palpable feeling of a presence throughout the building, even by children, who would run screaming from the downstairs bathroom claiming to have seen a little man there. A gentleman attending a meeting in the basement asked, quite out of the blue, if someone had recently died in that location.[282]

The Rogers Room of the library, which houses a significant history of the Rogers family, also includes a series of extremely lifelike portraits of H. H. Rogers, his mother, and his grandmother. Cold spots are often reported in this room, and the story goes that if a person is to speak directly to the portraits, the expressions will subtly change in reaction to the words being spoken.[283]

Author Tim Weisberg, who has conducted multiple investigations of the library, and has written about it in his book *Ghosts of the SouthCoast* (2010) and in various articles for a local newspaper, was standing in the Rogers Room attempting an interview with the portrait of Henry Huttleston Rogers during an investigation. At that moment, his colleague and fellow investigator Matt Costa burst into the room, declaring that he had not only witnessed one of the basement hallway lights going off and on by itself, but he had gotten the whole thing on video.[284]

Though the light switch turned on a pair of different lights in the hallway, the video Matt had recorded showed only a single light flickering on and off, something that neither Weisberg nor Costa could properly explain.[285]

The two men had also taken several photographs during that visit and noticed an orb floating in one of them. These spherical, transparent balls of light are often considered by paranormal investigators to be either remnants of pure energy being drawn by a nearby spirit, or evidence of a spirit attempting to manifest itself. Weisberg swore, when zooming in on this particular orb, that he could see the face of an elderly woman inside it. Another orb from a photo he took on another date appeared to have a clearly defined skull sitting in the centre of the image.[286]

Regardless of whether or not you believe there are deceased spirits wandering around this beautiful old library building, there is something timeless, precious, powerful, and inspiring about being able to stand near the stained-glass window and reflect on the image of Millicent.

The Millicent Library in Fairhaven, Massachusetts was funded and named after the daughter of principal founder, Henry Huddleston Rogers, who was a contemporary of such other notable Americans as Mark Twain, Helen Keller, and Booker T. Washington.[287]

As Mark Twain, dear friend of H. H. Huddleston, wrote in a February 22, 1894 letter to the officers of the Millicent Library, "It is the ideal, library, I think. Books are the liberated spirits of men, and should be bestowed in a heaven of light and grace and harmonious color and sumptuous comfort, like this, instead of in the customary kind of public library, with its depressing austerities and severities of form and furniture and decoration. A public library is the most enduring of memorials.... All other things which I have seen today must pass away and be forgotten, but there will still be a Millicent Library when by the mutations of language the books that are in it now will speak in a lost tongue to your posterity.[288]

THINGS THAT GO DING
IN THE NIGHT
Meridian-Lauderdale County Public Library
Meridian, Mississippi

There is something about the elevator in the Meridian-Lauderdale Library that just doesn't feel right, particularly on the second floor. Several staff members have experienced eerie feelings, especially when working alone in the library. Perhaps it has something to do with a former head librarian, who often stood at the top of the mezzanine watching her staff below in order to scold them if they did anything out of line.[289, 290]

Could she be running her library from beyond the grave?

In 1945, Jeanne Broach became the head librarian for Meridian Public Library, a role she retained for the next thirty years. She adored books, but also cherished efficiency with the same intense passion. She was considered a no-nonsense, stern woman, whose staff was always quite careful to toe the line.[291]

Of course, every rule has its exception, and there is a brief article that appeared as a short news tidbit in various newspapers in 1961 that demonstrates Broach's ability to turn the other cheek. Here is an example, from the *Biloxi Daily Herald*:

BOOK RETURNED 33 YEARS LATE

MERIDIAN, Miss. (AP) — Meridian library got back its book on "Agriculture and the Tariff" this week — 33 years late.

Librarian Jeanne Broach said the book was checked out March 2, 1928. It had long since been dropped from the records as a lost book.

The librarian said no fines were charged and the returnee was not identified. Fines would have totaled $201.96, she said.[292]

Broach retired on October 31, 1975, and died nearly a year later. It was almost as if, in retirement, she couldn't stand to be separated from the library that she had dedicated so much of her life to — and apparently, even death couldn't keep her away from her job. She seems to be connected, somehow, to the presence on the second floor, one that has the staff feeling strange and uneasy.

"It's mainly just eerie feelings," Reference Librarian Kevin Chatham said in a 2008 interview in the *Meridian Star*. "Once you step off that elevator at night, it's just sort of a heavy feeling."[293]

Library Director Steven McCartney has also heard strange, unexplainable noises coming from the second floor, and has felt unnatural cold spots in the library.[294]

"Whether it's a natural phenomenon or something else, I don't know," McCartney told a newspaper reporter in a 2008 interview. He has certainly felt cold for no apparent reason, though, and feels that it just might be because of the fact that everything in his office, with the exception of the filing cabinet, used to belong to Jeanne Broach. "Sometimes," McCartney said, "I look at her portrait, and I wonder if the girl is still around."[295, 296]

Speaking of the portrait, McCartney believes that if the power was out and it was the middle of the night, he wouldn't want to go into the same room where her likeness hangs.[297]

McCartney also recalled that one night when he was working alone in his office, he heard the distinct sound of the elevator ding, signalling that it was stopping to let someone off on his floor.[298] Grabbing his flashlight, McCartney rushed out into the library to search for an intruder, but there was nobody there. Furthermore, he discovered that the elevator hadn't moved at all.[299]

Other times, McCartney said, the elevator went down to either the first floor or the basement completely unaccompanied and entirely on its own. "That elevator's strange," he muttered.[300]

Whether or not Jeanne Broach actually does haunt the library, the employees who remember her are certainly haunted by the thought of her imposing presence, almost as if she might hold some sway over them from beyond the grave.[301]

Dr. Alan Brown, a professor at the University of West Alabama-Livingston and author of a number of books on haunted locales, visited the library one evening as part of an investigation. He wanted to test the theory that the ghost in the library might be that of another woman.[302]

Prior to the most recent incarnation of the Meridian-Lauderdale building, which opened in 1967, there was a personal home on that very same lot where a woman committed suicide. Dr. Brown believed it likely that her spirit was still wandering the grounds where she died.[303]

During the investigation, which involved a number of devices used to measure paranormal phenomenon, such as temperature gauges and EVP recorders, Dr. Brown waited until all the lights were turned off and addressed the spirits, asking them to give the team a sign of their presence. A strange noise was heard almost immediately. As the session continued, the sound repeated again, and the investigation team was eager at the thought that they had actually recorded one of the spirits. The excitement immediately waned, however, after they turned the lights back on and realized that the noise they heard had come from a nearby fuse box.[304]

Toward the end of the investigation, after discovering nothing that would suggest evidence of an actual haunting, the team were seated around the table when one of them remarked how cold the room suddenly seemed. Every person sitting around the table admitted that they could detect the temperature drop. But when they used their infrared thermometer to investigate the room's temperature, they were shocked to learn that it had not changed a single degree. As they were trying to figure out how that could be possible, one of the investigators felt something invisible brush against her cheek.[305]

Later that same evening, as they were beginning to wrap up for the night, librarian Kevin Chatham asked the group if they could hear the soft sound of a baby crying, which they couldn't. However, the next day Kevin spoke to another librarian about what he'd heard, and she admitted that she had heard the echoes of a baby's cries on several different occasions. Later, a former librarian admitted that she had heard the same sound one time when she had been alone in the library.[306]

Another eerie incident that occurred in the library involved a custodian named Nick, who was the only person in the library one Saturday morning in the fall of 2008.[307] Sitting in the break room on the second floor, Nick was startled to hear a woman's voice call out his name. He jumped to his feet, rushed out the break room door, and searched all throughout the second floor. He could not find anybody else there, and there was no explanation as to where the voice had come from.[308]

After that particular incident, he admitted to another staff member that he occasionally heard other strange noises in the library when he was by himself, such as the sound of books being shelved. He thought nothing of it until the incident when he'd heard that female voice calling out his name. Since that morning, he said, whenever he is working alone or taking a break, he turns the television on in the break room in order to drown out any unnerving sounds that he might hear.[309]

Despite the strange phenomena and the unexplainable sounds — the female voice, the crying baby, the sound of books being shelved, and the elevator dinging to announce its unmanned and uncalled arrival — no apparitions have ever been witnessed in the building. That fact, however, hasn't stopped an overwhelming eerie feeling from casting a shadow over the imaginations of those who work in the library alone.

HAVE GHOSTS, WILL TRAVEL

Parmly Billings Library

Billings, Montana

During the long history of the Billings Public Library, housed in several buildings over the years, various ghosts and eerie occurrences have been reported, including spirits that seem to have moved location along with the books.

The spectre of a little girl in a short frilly dress, which appears as if it is from the 1900s, has been spotted near a chair in the basement that came from the library's original location. A dark-haired woman has also been spotted in the basement, as well as on the third floor. A male ghost in jeans, a jean jacket, and work boots was spotted on the second floor, but vanished when a maintenance man approached him.[310]

Local historian Kevin Kooistra has spoken about the original location of the library, which at that time was housed in a castle. Speaking of the castle as one of the most interesting and significant buildings in Billings, Kooistra said it appears that the building has become quite haunted over the years.[311] In 1971, the Western Heritage Center, where Kooistra works as a community historian, moved into the building.[312]

"Staff members on many occasions have reported seeing figures in the hallways or hearing noise and coming out and seeing someone there," Kooistra said. "Downstairs in our dude ranch lobby area there's been at least a dozen sightings of this older gentleman in one of the chairs."[313]

Considering the trail of ghosts that this evolving and moving library has left behind, one can only imagine that, in its newest location, some legacy ghosts have hitched a ride along with some of the books. Perhaps some new spirits will also begin to make themselves known there, drawn by the library's long history of hauntings.

The original Billings Library was built in 1901 and named the Memorial Parmly Billings Library, in honour and memory of the son of Billings town founder, Frederick Billings. The original location was outgrown by the year 1969. Over time, the library has both continued to extend its operation and its innovation and made small tweaks in its name, from Memorial Parmly Billings Library to The Parmly Billings Library, and now to the Billings Public Library.[314]

A 66,000-square-foot, brand new Billings Public Library building, designed by Will Bruder & Partners, opened on January 6, 2014, with over 200,000 volumes in stock, community meeting rooms, study rooms, a café, and an atmosphere filled with natural light.[315]

THE GHOST WITH A LIBRARY CARD

Bernardsville Public Library
Bernardsville, New Jersey

A t over three hundred years old, Phyllis Bryam just might be the oldest library patron in the world. Since she is also dead, she is also probably the only ghost with her own library card.

Phyllis's story is a sad one. In the late 1700s, Phyllis's father, Captain John Parker, bought the Vealtown Tavern in Bernardsville, New Jersey, and moved in with her.[316] One of the local tenants at the inn was a handsome young doctor by the name of Bryam. After getting to know one another, Phyllis and Bryam fell in love and married. During their marriage, they continued to live in the home with the young woman's father.[317]

By 1777, the Vealtown Tavern was a popular place for American troops to stay during the Revolutionary War. One night, General Anthony Wayne was a guest at the inn. Finding that certain military documents had been stolen from his room,

Wayne questioned his hosts. That was when he spied a picture of Dr. Bryam and identified him as a Tory spy known as Aaron Wilde.[318] General Wayne sent a posse of troops to track down Dr. Bryam, and they cornered him in the nearby town of Blazure's Corner, where he was captured, tried, convicted, and hanged.[319]

Captain Parker requested that his son-in-law's body be delivered back to the tavern so that a proper burial could be arranged. The body was placed in a pine box, sealed, and delivered by a group of solders. The men dropped the pine box in the kitchen with a loud thud and marched right back out without saying a single word to anyone.[320]

As the legend goes, when Phyllis opened the pine box and observed the bug-eyed corpse of her dead husband, rope burns around his neck and his body battered and bruised, she became hysterical, suffering a nervous breakdown. Her heart-wrenching screams began almost immediately and went on for days.[321, 322]

What happened to poor Phyllis after that is unclear. However, the story continues one hundred years later, on the anniversary of Phyllis's viewing of her dead husband's body — long after the inn had been converted into a family home.

On a quiet afternoon, the woman who lived in the house was doing needlepoint in the front parlour while her toddler played on the floor with his wooden blocks. She heard a series of footfalls on the front porch and heard the door open, despite seeing with her own eyes that it was still closed. Confused and frightened, the woman picked up her son and hid them both behind a piece of furniture as the sound of the marching footsteps moved through her front room and into the kitchen, where there was a loud thud. The footsteps then proceeded to return back through the living room, out the front door, and down the front steps. A few moments later, she could hear the sound of someone coming down the front staircase and heading into the kitchen, followed by the sounds of wood being pried open and a series of horrific screams. At that point the woman bolted out the front door of the house and stayed with a neighbour until her husband returned home. Finding no signs of forced entry or evidence of heavy booted men and a hysterical woman in their home, they returned to a normal life and allegedly never saw or heard anything strange again.[323]

Speculation has it that the sounds this woman heard were the audible impressions of the traumatic moment when Phyllis discovered her husband's body. It is said that these same sounds repeat themselves only on the anniversary of the event.[324]

The Bernardsville Library eventually moved into the location, and when it was renovated in the 1970s, the disturbance seemed to trigger additional activity from Phyllis. There is one story of a teenaged employee who had returned to the library after her dinner break. As she looked up at the library, she noticed a young woman sitting on top of the table in the children's section and panicked, believing that they had accidentally locked a patron inside the building. She was frantically trying to get the door open when the supervising librarian arrived with the key. "Hurry!" she called out. "We've locked a girl in there!" The librarian simply smiled back at her as she unlocked the door. "That's just Phyllis," she said.[325]

Although Phyllis has never harmed or menaced anyone, the ghost apparently became curious about new technologies as they were introduced in the library. Objects have been moved and computer equipment was reported as being mysteriously tampered with over the years.[326] Occasional weeping has also been reported in the old section of the library, and the young woman's apparition has been seen floating through the old wing. There is even a videotape recording of a séance, held in 1987, which can be played by patrons in the Local History Room of the library.[327]

In her booklet *Phyllis—The Library Ghost?* Eileen Luz Johnston relays the story of a young boy who, in 1989, called his mother to the reading room in the library. He wanted her to look at the pretty woman standing in a long, flowing dress by the fireplace, but when the boy's mother entered the room, she could not see the woman, much to the boy's dismay.[328]

There is also a report from former Police Chief John Maddaluna, who encountered the library ghost as a rookie officer. Maddaluna, who was walking his beat in 1950, looked up after noticing movement out of the corner of his eye and spied a "female figure wearing a long, white dress that trailed down to the ground." Concerned that there was a break-in, Maddaluna shone his flashlight through the window and followed the female figure from room to room, uncertain as to what she was up to. When he reported the strange sight to his sergeant, the man just shrugged and told him that he had seen a ghost, which the sergeant himself had seen on several occasions.[329, 330]

The librarians, who have gotten used to having Phyllis around, have embraced her as if she were a regular patron of the library. Jean Hill, a volunteer at the library's Local History Room, said that Phyllis was not entered into their computers with the rest of their library patrons, "but her card is always available should she choose to use it."[331]

After the library moved to its new location, members of New Jersey Researchers of Paranormal Evidence (NJROPE) conducted several investigations of the old building, where Meli Melo, a retail store, now resides.[332] The team managed to come away with twenty-five hours of audio recordings, fifteen hours of video recordings, and 1,135 photographs. One of the photographs taken suggests the shadow mass of a man and a partial manifestation of a woman.[333] Their research and follow-up unveiled a former librarian by the name of Clara who communicated with staff of Meli Melo through their computer, with the following words appearing on the screen: "I am CLARA!!! Please HELP Help!!!"[334]

This more recent investigation of the premises found no evidence of Phyllis. Is it possible that she followed the library to its new home — perhaps to keep using the library card in her name?

INTERNATIONAL

GHOSTS OF THE ROYAL LIBRARY

Windsor Castle Library

Berkshire, England

At more than one thousand years old, Windsor Castle is touted as the oldest and largest occupied castle in the world. It also might just hold the record for being occupied with the most ghosts.[1]

Originally constructed around 1070 by William the Conqueror, the castle is still a working royal palace, has been the family home to generations of kings and queens and is the official residence of Her Majesty the Queen. The Queen occasionally hosts "dine and sleep" events with ambassadors, high commissioners, or the heads of commonwealth nations staying overnight, having dinner and being shown a special display of items from the Royal Library.[2]

Of course, not often displayed during these overnight visits are the ghosts of the many people who have died inside the castle over the hundreds of years it has stood.

The ghost of Anne Boleyn, a woman who was beheaded in London Tower after claims by King Henry VIII of treason, adultery, and witchcraft, is often seen peering out the windows of the Dean's Cloister. The ghost of King Henry himself is occasionally seen anxiously pacing about the castle and shouting furiously. Ghostly footsteps are often heard echoing in the stairway of Curfew Tower, and in 1936 workmen reported seeing the ghostly figure of Queen Victoria waving her arms at them and moaning loudly as she strode toward them.[3, 4]

While those and so many other ghosts are reported in this thousand-year-old castle, there are three of primary concern for this book: the ghosts that haunt the castle library.

Queen Elizabeth I, who was said to have had a premonition about her own death, is seen in spectral form every March 24, the anniversary of her death at the age of sixty-nine in 1603. Elizabeth had an ongoing strange feeling that if she were ever to take off her Coronation ring, she would die. The ring, which she never removed, had grown into the flesh of her finger and advisors suggested she remove it. She did, and she died a week later.[5]

A guard relayed the experience of following the former queen into the library and was astonished when the female form of Her Majesty suddenly disappeared, and the late princess Margaret, sister to Queen Elizabeth II, reported seeing the woman's ghost standing among the shelves of books in the library. King George III claimed to have engaged in a long conversation with a ghostly woman dressed all in black who claimed to be "married to England" and have the name of Elizabeth, and one hundred years after that, Edward VII is said to have had an eerie night-time encounter with a woman in black who resembled Elizabeth I.[6, 7]

The sounds of Elizabeth's high heels are said to have been heard on bare floorboards in the castle's library. Lieutenant Carr Glyn claimed in 1897 that he was sitting in the library one night, idly looking at a book, when he heard the distinct tapping of high-heeled shoes. As he listened, they become louder and more distinct, coming obviously closer. When he looked up from his book, he immediately recognized the woman coming toward him from across the library as Queen Elizabeth I from her portrait. He watched her glide past him and remarked that she had been close enough that he could have reached out and touched her, which he didn't. Instead, he watched her walk away and into an inner room of the library, where she disappeared.[8]

King George III, who suffered from bouts of mental illness, used to be confined to a room directly below the library during his occasional "periods of madness." The man's ghost has been reported as peering mournfully in through library windows and doors.[9]

And King Charles I, who was beheaded in 1649 after being accused of treason, has reportedly been seen standing near a table in the library.[10]

It is doubtful that, during the aforementioned overnight visits, these tales are among the things shared in the library; if so, one can assume that the guests would be quite unlikely to have any sort of restful sleep, lying awake and wondering if that odd noise they heard in the thick of night were some standard noise made by mortal method or perhaps caused by one of the many spirits roaming the castle after dark.

THE WHITE LADY OF
THE HAUNTED BOOKSHOP

The Haunted Bookshop / Sarah Key Books

Cambridge, England

Sarah Key Books (also known as The Haunted Bookshop) is only like the store in Christopher Morley's novel of the same name in that the owner has a true passion for books. Nestled in a quiet passage in the heart of the City of Cambridge, Sarah Key Books has occupied The Haunted Bookshop since 1993.[11]

The inspiration for the book shop's name came from the legend of a presence at the store known as The White Lady. Smelling of violets and swathed all in white, this spirit is said to wander the creaky stairs between the first and second floors and put a fright into those who happen upon her. Historic accounts of the building as an alehouse suggest that this woman might be a drunken reveller's wife, coming forth to call him home. That alone would put a chill into the heart of a happy barfly, but the presence brings chills into those she encounters in the dark dim realm of the stairways of the building.[12]

The shop specializes in children's and illustrated books, and though it might at first seem disorganized and a bit neglected, there is indeed a place for everything.[13] For example, the first floor is devoted almost entirely to huge piles of poetry, threatening to collapse one way or the other, and the second floor is dedicated to juvenile fiction.[14]

Perhaps in ode to its name, or perhaps as a business ploy to cater to the streams of tourists who are dropped off at the building as part of a walking ghost tour of Cambridge, there is an entire wall dedicated to ghost stories and legends.[15]

LORD COMBERMERE'S CHAIR

Combermere Abbey Library

Whitchurch, England

Perhaps the most famous library ghost ever is that of Lord Combermere. His spectral image appeared, sitting in his favourite chair in the library of his ancestral home, in a photograph in 1891.

Founded in 1133 as a Cistercian monastery by Hugh de Malbanc, Lord of Nantwich, Combermere Abbey is a complex of both medieval and sixteenth-century buildings that overlook a 143-acre lake.[16] After Henry VIII enacted the Dissolution of the Monasteries in 1536, only the abbot's lodge, which was constructed in 1503, remained to be presented to the Cotton family, who owned the estate until 1919.[17]

Colonel Wellington Stapleton-Cotton, the second Viscount Lord Combermere, was a British soldier and politician who died in 1891 after being struck by one of London's very first electrically powered motor cabs. Even though his funeral took place about four miles away at the time, Combermere apparently thought it was important to return to his library, which Sybell Corbet inadvertently captured in a picture.[18, 19]

The photograph clearly shows the image of an older gentleman seated in the chair, with his head, collar, and right arm resting on the chair's armrest, clearly visible. The man's legs and lower body are mostly absent in the photograph, which is interesting, as when Lord Combermere was struck, the damage to his legs was so severe that, had he lived, he likely never would have been able to walk.[20]

Photo of Combermere Abbey library and Lord Combermere's ghost, taken by Sybell Corbet in 1891.

Corbet had intended to capture a simple photograph of the beautiful library. She set the camera near the oak chair — Lord Combermere's favourite — and set the exposure to approximately fifteen minutes. While Corbet stated that she was the only one going in and out of the library at the time, she did admit that she may have left the room for several minutes while the photograph was being captured.[21, 22] This has led to speculation that perhaps a man came into the room during the exposure, but this theory has been refuted by family members, who said the servants had all been attending the funeral. In addition, none of them would have looked old enough to be mistaken for Lord Combermere.[23]

In Sir William Barrett's 1918 book, *On the Threshold of the Unseen: An Examination of the Phenomenon of Spiritualism and the Evidence for Survival After Death*, he describes his attempt to replicate the photo:

> In reply to my enquiries Miss C. informed me the exposure of the plate was lengthy some 15 minutes, and that she had for a short time left the empty room during the exposure of the plate. I thought it possible one of the men servants had come in and seated himself in the chair until he heard Miss C. returning. Accordingly I made a photographic test of this surmise. Exposing a half-plate in the panelled library of the house of my friend the late Mr. Titus Salt, where I happened to be staying, I asked his eldest son, then a youth, to walk into the room, sit down in the oak arm chair, cross and un-cross his legs, move his head slightly, and then walk out of the room.
>
> This was done and we developed the photo-graph together; when lo! there came out almost a duplicate of the Combermere

photo-graph, a shadowy rather aged man with no legs seated in the chair, and no signs of any-one coming into or leaving the room. I wrote a paper on the whole matter and published it, with a reproduction of the two photographs, in the "Journal of the Society for Psychical Research" for December, 1895.

There I thought the matter ended, with a young footman as the soi-disant Lord Combermere; but I found that Miss C. and some others of the family strongly dissented from my view. They had closely examined their servants and had reason to believe that the denial, by the footman and others, — of any visit to the room at the time when the ex-posure took place, — was perfectly correct and straightforward.[24]

The photo of Lord Combermere's ghost is one of the world's most commonly cited and iconic photographs of ghosts. To think, all because the man couldn't bear to leave his favourite library chair.

MACABRE SECRETS OF
THE MUNICIPAL PALACE

Leeds Central Library

Leeds, England

D ark, menacing shadows are said to lurk among the aisles of books in the old Victorian building that houses the Leeds Central Library.

Since its opening in 1884, the Leeds Central Library has been affectionately dubbed "The Municipal Palace," with its extravagant stairwell in what used to be the building's main entrance made of Devonshire marble. This elegant stone staircase has been the site of more than one macabre event, and continues to draw intrigued visitors to the building.[25, 26]

A former employee of the library plunged from the fourth storey to his death. Though the reason is unexplained, there has been much speculation about how the accident happened, even questions about whether or not it was an accident at all.[27]

Shortly after the library opened, a man committed suicide near the same spot, and his ghost is said to roam the halls. His floating presence has been seen in the main hallway as well as the third floor reading room and is accompanied by a dark and eerie feeling. It is said that the spirit's temper is short and quite violent.[28]

An overwhelming feeling of being watched has often been reported by visitors to the old Victorian building, and patrons have reported the mysterious sound of footsteps trailing them up the stairs, despite finding nobody there when they turned around.[29] Odd anomalies of light have also been reported in the library, and dark, menacing figures have been seen skulking around the aisles.[30]

The library has held overnight ghost hunts catering to those with more macabre tastes, but the library itself maintains a well-balanced approach to serving its citizens. *The Secret Library*, home to Leeds Libraries heritage blog, is a wonderful celebration of insights into the history, magnificent architecture, and cherished stories concerning the old building.

Constructed between 1878 and 1884 and located on Calverley Street in Leeds, Leeds Central Library houses the city library's single largest general lending and reference collection and also includes specialist departments to assist with enquiries and research. The location also houses an Art Library, Music and Performing Arts department, Business and IP Centre, Leeds and Local Family History department, and the adjoining Leeds City Art Gallery.[31, 32]

STERNBERG'S GHOST

Leeds Library
Leeds, England

The ghost of former librarian Vincent Thomas Sternberg is said to appear in, and occasionally be heard among, the stacks at Leeds Library.

In May of 1880, Ian Young Walker Macalister (better known as John Macalister) became librarian; this was a position he was to hold for seven years. However, a story that Macalister shared regarding an experience in 1884 has far outlasted the man's seven-year term there.[33]

Macalister was working late into the evening in March 1884, when he realized that he had stayed so long that he ran the risk of missing the last evening train home.[34] Gathering together his things and quickly snatching a lamp, Macalister rushed from his office and through the darkness of the library. At the end of the passageway, he spied, in the faint illumination from his lamp, a man's face.[35] Believing the stranger to be an intruder, Macalister dashed back into his office, retrieved a loaded revolver, and went back out to confront the burglar. He continued to shout warnings as he crept forward, the revolver in one hand and the lamp in the other. But there was no answer.[36]

Then, just as he was approaching a bookcase, the same face appeared from around the side of it.[37] Hairless, and with deep-set, heavy-shadowed eye sockets, the pale face seemed to be glaring back at him; however, with the eyes so deeply hidden in the shadow, Macalister couldn't be sure. As he took several steps around the corner of the bookshelves, he could also make out the body of a tall, old man that seemed to be spiralling its way out of the end of the bookcase itself.[38]

Macalister shook his head in amazement at the bizarre sight and watched as the man turned his back and, with an odd, shuffling gait, walked quickly down the aisle toward the lavatory.[39] Following the man's path, Macalister entered the small lavatory to discover the man had completely vanished.[40]

"I confess," Macalister was quoted as saying when he later recollected the incident, "I began to experience for the first time what novelists describe as an 'eerie' feeling."[41]

A local priest by the name of Charles Hargrove identified the man Macalister described as Vincent Sternberg, the librarian who had been Macalister's predecessor.[42] Sternberg had apparently lost his hair and gained a strange shuffling gait as the after-effect of an accidental gunpowder blast.[43]

Following that incident, various librarians working in the library after dark reported lamps being mysteriously extinguished and then re-lit, as well as the reverberant echoes of what people believed were "Sternberg's gong" — a reference to an old gong the librarian kept on one particular library table that he would strike in order to summon an assistant librarian.[44]

A séance of sorts was later held, with the use of Sternberg's gong to signal the typical "yes" or "no" responses. It was learned, among other things, that Sternberg, who didn't believe in the afterlife, was quite miserable in his new unearthly position.[45]

Perhaps Sternberg was more frustrated that he had become known as a paranormal curiosity rather than for the positive contribution he had made as both a librarian and as a scholar. In 2013, Dr. Jonathan Roper gave a series of university talks explaining that Vincent Thomas Sternberg should have been remembered as the first author to use the word "folklore" in the title of a full-length book, or as one of the few successful collectors of Märchen in mid-nineteenth-century England, rather than simply being remembered as the long-suffering ghost of Leeds Library.

Founded in 1768, Leeds Library (not to be confused with Leeds Central Library) is the oldest surviving example of a proprietary subscription library (one that relies on a membership based on annual paid subscriptions) in the UK.[46, 47]

The library has a stock of over 140,000 books, with a particularly strong collection of literature, history, travel, and biography, and continues to add between 1,000 to 1,500 new items each year to its growing collection.[48]

THE BOOK-LOVING GHOST
OF FELBRIGG HALL

Felbrigg Hall

Norfolk, England

Felbrigg Hall, a seventeenth-century country estate, is well-known for its beautiful gothic library.

Originally owned by the Felbrigg family, Felbrigg became the long-time home of the Wyndham family for approximately four hundred years before the home was passed into National Trust.[49]

Although the Wyndham family no longer resides in the building, legend has it that there is one book-loving family member who forever remains, often seen among the books in the building's library.

William Wyndham III was a notable statesman and orator. But he was also a notable book lover, and that is what led to his tragic demise.[50]

On a summer evening in 1809, Wyndham noticed a fire at a building on Conduit Street, near the home of his friend Robert

North. Having been an admirer of North's lavish and expensive library, Wyndham immediately rushed into the home and began an operation to ensure the rescue of the entire library from the damaging fire.[51] Most of the valuable manuscripts were saved in the endeavour; but Wyndham fell during the incident and severely bruised his hip. The bruise turned bad and eventually led to the man's death just a few weeks later.[52, 53]

Since then, Wyndham's ghost has often been witnessed sitting in a chair in the library by the fire, engrossed in a book, or standing over a table as if surveying the marvellous collection of tomes.

In November 1972, David Muffon was working in the library, filing paperwork on behalf of National Trust, who had acquired the estate. Suddenly, he noticed what he described as "a gentleman sitting in the armchair by the fireplace reading books. It was so natural I thought nothing about it. After about fifteen seconds he put the book down beside him on the table and faded away."[54]

When Muffon later asked the old family butler if the house had any ghosts, he was told that the ghost of William Wyndham often sat in the armchair on the far side of the fireplace. For many years the butler had set out books, specifically those given to Wyndham by his friend Samuel Johnson, on the table for the ghost to read.[55]

Talk about a dedicated butler, providing such thoughtful service even after the family's — and one particular bibliophile's — departure.

Felbrigg Hall is a seventeenth-century country home located in Felbrigg, Norfolk, England. Noted for its Jacobean architecture and Georgian interior, the building stood at the centre of one of the largest estates in Norfolk, and today covers some 1,760 acres of parkland that includes the 520-acre Great Wood, which continues to shelter the home.[56]

Felbrigg's current Gothic library is one of the home's exquisite attractions. This room, which was made into the library by William Wyndham II between 1752 and 1755, contains approximately five thousand books, including a copy of Dr. Johnson's famous dictionary. The oldest book in the room dates from 1509. Every book has been read.[57]

Just off the library is the book room, which contains various exhibits, such as one on the women of Felbrigg, the wives and daughters who are often overlooked in much of the estate's history. Among the bookish treasures people can see are: Katherine Wyndham's well-thumbed book of plays; Rachel Ketton's diaries, which offer a fascinating insight into the lives of a Norfolk family; and Emily Ketton-Cremer's beekeeping books and album of postcards.[58]

THE BLUE MAN

Arundel Castle

Sussex, England

Arundel Castle, boasting more than a thousand years of history, is believed to be home to four different spirits. These include one thought to be the first Earl of Arundel himself, who roams the castle. Legend has it that his ghost is forever keeping watch over the building that he played a major role in founding.[59]

The second ghost is that of a young woman dressed in white. She is believed to have committed suicide in response to a badly ended love affair by leaping from Arundel's Hiornes tower, which is behind the castle within Arundel Park. Often seen on moonlit nights and dressed in white, she is a haunting and sad spectre.

The third reported ghost is not the ghost of a human. This one is instead a bird, and appears in the guise of a white owl. Often seen at one of the windows of the castle, usually just before someone who either lived in the castle or was closely associated with residents of the castle has died, this ghost is believed to be the harbinger of death.[60]

For the purpose of this book, the "Blue Man" ghost is one of the most interesting.

Favouring the library, accounts of the "Blue Man" have been reported since the 1630s. Within the library, which is renowned as one of the finest Gothic rooms in the country, this ghost is seen floating about the room. At times, people have even witnessed him browsing through the books.[61, 62] Consistently described as wearing a blue silk suit, the "Blue Man" sometimes appears to be searching through the books themselves for some elusive passage.[63]

OPEN TO ALL

State Library of Victoria
Melbourne, Australia

The State Library of Victoria is open to all, including, apparently, preternatural visitors.

Though there are no stories of anyone having died in the library during its long history, there are still many tales of ghosts that are whispered about among its hallowed halls.

A ghostly woman dressed in red wanders among the bookshelves, and spectral orbs have also been reported in the library stairwells. A piano plays all on its own, as if the keys are being pressed by unseen fingers. In 2010, Isabel Dunstan wrote about her tour of the library for *Time Out Melbourne*, in which she shared her tour guide's insistence that, even though no death had ever occurred inside the library, it is haunted by a ghost that plays the piano at night. The guide had been told by managers that they had actually seen visions of the ghost, and electricians refused to work alone in the building at night.[64]

Other ghosts that have been reported at this library include an elderly gentlemen who has been seen wandering the halls, and whose spectral form is regularly reported among the music stacks. There have also been reports of a poltergeist or several noisy ghosts making a ruckus in the newspaper room.[65]

Perhaps the most intriguing ghost is one who has been given the name of Grace, and is believed to be the spirit of a former librarian. Grace, who appears in a white dress, is said to keep a matronly eye on the children's books in the Art Collection. It is believed that her fondness for children's literature and the young patrons are what keep her there, forever caring for that special section of the library.[66]

The State Library of Victoria was conceived by founder Sir Redmond Berry as "the people's university" and meant to be a place where the world's knowledge and information would be freely available to every citizens of the colony of Victoria, regardless of their financial resources or their social status.[67]

The library was one of the first free public libraries in the world and, through the many changes, additions, and new implementations it has seen, the library has successfully pursued their ambition, offering services to a continually growing number of Victorians.

That defining concept guided the library from its foundation in 1854 through the more than 150 years of its history. The current mission of the library reads "We want to be a place where all Victorians can discover, learn, create, and connect. We want to be a cultural and heritage destination for Victorians, and a catalyst for generating new knowledge and ideas."[68]

A TREASURE OF INFINITE HAUNTS

The Haunted Bookshop [69]
Melbourne, Australia

Although there are not many ghost stories about Drew Stinson's The Haunted Bookshop in Melbourne, Australia, I would be remiss not to mention it as an amazing resource for almost anything mystical and paranormal.

With a book line specializing in topics such as ghosts, witchcraft, vampires, the psychic, aliens, angels, and the gothic, the bookstore boasts Australia's largest range of occult books and has been called "a destination for curious shoppers in search of a thrill" by *Melbourne Age*.

The store contains a broad selection of genuine alchemy, gothic pendants, rings, earrings, chokers and bracelets, as well as a full programming lineup of thirty-minute *HauntedTV* episodes presented by Drew Stinson and the Haunted Australia team of investigators and psychics.

The bookshop is also home to Melbourne's oldest and most famous ghost tours, having been established in 1997, and each tour is presented by bookstore owner and Foxtel's *Haunted Australia* TV presenter Drew Stinson.

The tours take participants into an eye-opening look at the ghosts and graveyards that the city has to offer; they cover the ghosts of the State Library, which is allegedly the most haunted building in Melbourne due to the ghosts having traversed across the street from the now-demolished Queen Victoria Hospital, as well as the ghost of an old regular at the Treasury Casino who is claimed to be responsible for the mysterious movement of an expensive decanter of whisky. Participants also learn about the ghost of a man seen in a bloody apron, known as "The Butcher," who has been spotted haunting the local morgue.[70]

Other ghosts mentioned on the tour include that of a man who was decapitated in an unfortunate accident involving horses that were spooked and whose ghost has been spotted in the basement of a local hotel, and the ghost of a former prison officer who still patrols the cells at night, shining a spectral flashlight in on prisoners and pulling back the eyeholes in the cell doors.[71]

The bookstore itself, of course, offers up a ghost not often spoken about who is known as "Donald." This ghost made his presence known when owner Drew Stinson, who is also an author, historian, ghost-researcher, and tour guide, conducted séances with a clairvoyant. Stinson claims that Donald still appears to some people, from time to time, on the rear stairway and out the back.[72]

So whether you are in the mood for a tour, something gothic to wear, or an eerie read, if you're in Melbourne you should make sure to make The Haunted Bookshop one of the stops on your tour.

THE HIDDEN NOTE IN MARSH'S LIBRARY

Marsh's Library

Dublin, Ireland

There is a forlorn ghost in Marsh's Library, perpetually searching through the books, looking for a hidden note from a loved one.

Marsh's Library was founded in 1701 by Archbishop Narcissus Marsh (1638–1713), and is one of a very few buildings in Dublin that is still used for its original purpose. Born in Hannington, Wiltshire, Marsh was educated at Oxford University where he studied old philosophy, mathematics, and oriental languages. He became a clergyman in the Church of England and was later appointed provost at Trinity College in Dublin.[73, 74]

Shortly after his arrival in Dublin, Marsh learned that while Trinity College had a library available to students and staff, there was no public library available to the rest of its citizens. His desire to open a public library became a reality when he was appointed Archbishop of Dublin in 1694. The palace he lived in had enough land available that he could easily build a library on the grounds.[75] The "Rules of the Library" were set forth on October 8, 1713:

> Concerning Those Who shall be allowed to study in the said Library, We order and appoint that all Graduates and Gentlemen shall have free access to the said Library on the Dayes and Hours before determined, Provided They behave Themselves well, give place and pay due respect to their Betters, But in Case any person shall carry Himself otherwise (which We hope will not happen) We order Him to be excluded, if after being admonished He does not mend His Manners.[76]

One might only hope that such a blatantly laid-out statement existed on many public buildings and social media websites today.

Narcissus Marsh died in 1713, and is buried just outside his library, in the grounds of St. Patrick's Cathedral. Some say that his ghost has been seen in the library, and there may be a good reason for it. Marsh made a diary entry on September 10, 1695, after his niece, Grace — whom he had raised almost as if she were his own child — married a sea captain of whom Marsh disapproved.[77, 78]

> This evening betwixt 8 and 9 of the clock at night my niece Grace Marsh (not having the fear of God before her eyes) stole privately out of my house at St. Sepulchre's and (as is reported) was that night married to Chas. Proby vicar of

Castleknock in a Tavern and was bedded there
with him — Lord consider my affliction.[79]

Legend has it that, before she ran off to be married, Grace
wrote a note to her uncle in which she pleaded for his forgiveness, slipping it into one of his books in the library. However,
Marsh never knew about the note, and allegedly died with the
thought of his lost niece weighing on his heart. Only after death,
when his spirit learned she had hidden a note away for him,
did he return in spectral form to spend an eternity searching
through the books of the library, looking for the note she had
tucked away for him.[80]

> The website for Marsh's Library invites people to "step
> into the Eighteenth Century" with a blurb that reads:
> "Unchanged for three centuries, this perfectly pre-
> served library of the early Enlightenment, with its orig-
> inal oak bookcases, houses more than 25,000 rare and
> fascinating books."[81]
>
> For 100 years after it opened, Marsh's Library was
> the only free library in Dublin and the only public library
> in Ireland for nearly 150 years.

OLD JACOBUS OF RAMMERSCALES

Rammerscales Mansion Library

Lockerbie, Scotland

Rammerscales House is a classic mid-eighteenth-century mansion near Lockerbie, Scotland. It boasts an impressive library, featuring not only a unique collection of books, but a resident spirit, eternally hiding in his manor.[82]

Dr. James Mounsey, who completed the home in 1768, made much of his fortune in Russia serving as a physician. He was there from 1736 to 1762, before returning to Scotland after the Tsar Peter III was murdered. Fearing for his own safety, Mounsey allegedly faked his own death and stayed holed up at Rammerscales, where he had constructed two doors to every room of the house, so he could have a clear escape route should he ever be cornered.[83]

Mounsey died, still in fear, in 1773. Despite the attention he paid to having a wealth of escape routes, it appears that his spirit never did find its way out. Alternatively, it is entirely possible that Mounsey, still scared of being discovered, chose to remain hidden in the safety of his home for all of eternity.

His ghost, nicknamed "Old Jacobus," is said to mostly haunt the mansion's library. It was reported that a teacher and students who were staying there were so frightened by the ghost in the library that they instead felt safer sleeping in the stables.[84]

GHOST IN A DARK GREEN JACKET

Brodick Castle Library

Brodick, Scotland

With a history that spans as far back as the fifth century, Brodick Castle has, not surprisingly, been the location for many a ghostly legend.

A Grey Lady has been seen wandering the castle, especially in the kitchen and lower corridor area. She is believed to be a servant girl dating back from the Cromwell era. A White Hart stag appeared to some eyewitnesses on the castle grounds, and a dark shape has been noted as appearing on the main stairwell.[85]

There has also been an apparition of an old man, in a dark green, velvet coat, seen sitting in the library, as well as moving through in the long corridor leading up to the library. When spotted in the corridor, his apparition immediately disappears. However, despite his affinity for the collection of books, there aren't many clues in the castle's history as to who he might actually be.[86]

THE MYSTERIOUS BOOK OF ANTIQUITIES AND CURIOSITIES

York Museum Library[87]

York, England

One Sunday evening in 1953 at the York Museum, a care-taker by the name of George Jonas was doing his rounds. He was checking the building when he encountered an odd man dressed in early-twentieth-century garb that included narrow trousers, a frock coat, and elastic-sided boots.

Jonas addressed the strange man, who ignored him and brushed right past. The man headed over to search through books in the religious section, muttering the words "I must find it," repeatedly. As Jonas slowly approached, he reached out a hand, intending to tap the man on the shoulder and secure his attention. However, the moment that his fingers should have come in contact with the man's shoulder, the stranger imme-diately vanished and the book he had been leafing through fell to the floor.

Disturbed, confused, and somewhat frightened, Jonas left the library, locked up the building, and returned home.

The next morning, he informed the library curator of the uncanny experience he had had the night before, and the two returned to the spot in the library where it had happened. The book, entitled *Antiquities and Curiosities of the Church* and edited by William Andrews, a well-known historian, was still lying on the floor where Jonas had watched it fall the night before.

One month later, on another Sunday night, Jonas saw the same strange man. This time, the man moved across the hall and glided straight through the locked doors to the library. However, when Jonas unlocked the doors and checked inside, the man was nowhere to be found. He had, like the week before, disappeared into thin air.

Another four weeks passed, and this time Jonas and a colleague awaited the return of the strange paranormal visitor. While the man never showed, both men noticed that the room had inexplicably plunged into extreme cold. Then, one of the books floated out from the shelves, opened, and the pages quickly shuffled. As the men moved closer, the book fell straight to the floor.

As the legend goes, the strange old man and the levitating book are only ever seen on Sundays, typically spaced out in the same four-week pattern. Investigations by groups such as the Society of Physical Research and the York Philosophical Society, as well as ad hoc gatherings of individuals, have often resulted in no accompanying manifestations.

The theory is that the supernatural visitor, who constantly looks for and shuffles through this particular book, is that of Alderman Edward Wooler, a historian and antiquarian who passed away in the 1920s.

The occasional sighting of the ghostly visitor and the dropping book continued until 1978, when the curator at the time decided to donate the book to the York City Library's collection of rare and valuable volumes.

Since then, the book is reported to have done nothing more than sit quietly in its shelf. The strange male visitor has neither been spotted in the original library, nor, apparently, in his precious text's new home.

THE NUN IN BLUE

Morelia Public Library, Michoacan's University of San Nicolas de Hidalgo

Morelia, Mexico

The Michoacan's University of San Nicolas de Hidalgo houses a public library, which was established in 1930. It is located in what once was The Temple of the Society of Jesus, and this baroque-style building has more than 22,000 texts dating from the fifteenth to the nineteenth century, as well as a nun who can't seem to leave.[88]

The history of the building is what leads to the mysterious phenomenon that has been reported there. Back in the sixteenth century, deceased nuns were buried in the floors and walls of the building. It is also reported that the librarian's desk sits atop a burial slab from a more recent twentieth-century burial.[89]

As reported in a 1996 *El Norte* newspaper article, a library worker requested a transfer out of the building to another area after feeling a presence standing behind her, followed by a startling feeling of someone breathing into her ear. She reported being gripped by a chill and unable to turn around, she was completely rooted to the spot.[90]

"When I leave the building," Library Director Rigoberto Cornejo said in an *El Norte* interview, "I feel the sensation of someone following me." Cornejo — a scholar who does not believe in the supernatural and desires some sort of logical or rational way to explain his experiences — went on to state that he could even hear footfalls behind him as he wandered the stacks. Yet nobody was there when he looked.[91]

In 1984, a group of high school students captured something startling in a photo taken among the library stacks while they were on a photographic tour of the building. There was an eerie silhouette in one of their photos, projected onto a row of books. When the photo was shown to the library staff, they identified the shadow in the photo as being that of the "nun in blue," who they said had haunted the library for multiple generations.[92]

THE RESTLESS LIBRARIAN
Africana Library
Kimberley, South Africa

Ghost tours of Kimberley, South Africa, include the Africana Library on their many stops, where the tale of the restless spirit of the building's first librarian is shared.

Bertrand Dyer sailed from England to South Africa in the late nineteenth century and established himself as a librarian. He took his role quite seriously, sorting and referencing the books in the collection, which, even then, was estimated as one of the world's largest. He also began the process of restoring and preserving its most valuable pieces.[93]

It is said that Dyer also fiddled with the account books, perhaps in an overenthusiastic passion for the library's well-being. When his deceptive practice was discovered, he committed suicide by consuming arsenic.[94] It allegedly took him three long and miserable days to die from the poison.[95]

Today, people report that they have heard the footfalls of a man pacing the library from room to room. Could it be echoes of the concerned, confused, and cornered Dyer, in the frantic moments after his deception was discovered and before he decided to take his own life?[96]

Many people have seen a man in period dress matching the description of Dyer walking up and down the corridors of the library. Other visitors have seen books inexplicably crashing to the floor, and some have heard teacups tinkling at precisely 4:00 p.m.[97] Obviously he cannot leave the library he cared so much about, even to his own detriment.

The building that houses Kimberley Africana Library first opened on July 23, 1887 as the Kimberley Public Library, an institution that initiated the collection of rare books and Africana.[98]

When the Kimberley Public Library moved to its new location in 1984, the old library building was restored and refurbished. It opened its doors to the public as an exclusively Africana research library in 1986, open to all bona fide researchers.[99]

This library, which houses one of the largest and most valuable collections of old books and manuscripts in the world, comprises books, manuscripts, maps, and photographs. There is other documentary material on Kimberley, the North Cape, the Diamond Fields, geology, archaeology, and thousands of items celebrating the region's past and its role in the history of both South Africa and Africa at large. The highlights of the collection are books and pamphlets in indigenous languages that date from 1826, records by early European travellers to the region, and materials dealing with the Anglo-Boer War (1899–1902).[100, 101]

WHEN A BOOK GETS UNDER YOUR SKIN

Multiple Locations

E very book lover knows that there are books that can really get under your skin. Either you are so engaged in the book that you simply can't put it down, or something about the book really strikes a nerve and you just can't stop thinking about it after you finish.

But sometimes books get under the skin in a more literal sense.

Anthropodermic bibliopegy is the practice of binding books in human skin. It is quite rare, particularly today, but it dates back as early as the thirteenth century, with one of the earliest reputed examples being a French Bible.[102]

The Harvard University Library system reportedly has at least three books in its archives that are bound by human skin. One book, in the Elihu Reading Room, has been described as "subdued yellow, with sporadic brown and black splotches like an old banana." Entitled "Practicarum quaestionum circa leges regias ..." it is a Spanish Law book that dates back to 1605. [103] There is an inscription on the last page that reads:

> "the bynding of this booke is all that remains of my dear friende Jonas Wright, who was flayed alive by the Wavuma on the Fourth Day of August, 1632. King Mbesa did give me the book, it being one of poore Jonas chiefe possessions, together with ample of his skin to bynd it. Requiescat in pace."[104]

Harvard apparently acquired the book for $42.50 from a rare book dealer in New Orleans in 1945. The current worth of the book (regardless of the human skin), is estimated to be somewhere between $500 and $1,000.[105]

Interestingly, DNA tests in 1992 proved inconclusive in regards to the book binding's origin, but an article published by Daniel Lovering in April 2014 reported that scientific testing of nine different samples from the book revealed it to be bound in sheepskin and that the glue from the binding consisted of cattle and pig collagen.[106, 107]

Two other books allegedly bound in human skin reside in the Countaway Library of Medicine and the Houghton Collection, respectively: a 1597 French translation of Ovid's *Metamorphoses*, with the pencilled inscription, "bound in human skin" written on the inside cover, and a collection of essays by Arsène Houssaye meditating on the human spirit, entitled "Des destinées de l'ame ...", which supposedly came with a typed memorandum that reads, "the back of the unclaimed body of a woman patient in a French mental hospital who died suddenly of apoplexy."[108]

The Surgeon's Hall Museum in Edinburgh has, amongst its collection, a book smaller than the size of a standard mass market paperback, with the words "EXECUTED 28 JAN 1829" and "BURKE'S SKIN POCKET BOOK" embossed on the cover. This particular book is allegedly bound in the flesh of William Burke, who — along with a co-conspirator who turned Kings's evidence on him to escape punishment — drugged and killed sixteen people for the purpose of selling their bodies to an anatomist.[109]

Another ne'er-do-well, whose legacy survives not only in the skin wrapped around a book, but also as the subject of the book itself, is James Allen and his 1837 book *Hic Liber Waltonis Cute Compactus Est*. It documents the memoirs of this notorious highwayman and bank robber. At sentencing for his execution, Allen decreed that the book be made and given to his attempted last victim as a token of respect for surviving Allen's assault. This particular book resides in the Boston Athanaeum in Boston, Massachusetts.[110]

Considering the various forms and formats that books have been available in over the years — scrolls, hardcover, trade paperback, mass market, audio, and e-book — perhaps those of us who find ourselves drawn by the mystique of books are a little bit relieved that this morbid practice never really caught on.

AFTERWORD

When I was writing this book, I found myself lost in the bookish locales I was exploring and, when I was less than halfway through the writing process I realized that there would be no way for me to be able to capture or tell them all. I thus did my best to collect several lists so that other places not covered in detail could at least be alluded to or mentioned. If you found your own favourite local bookish haunt was not mentioned or you have a tale to share, there might always be a follow-up and I would appreciate hearing from you. My email address is mark@markleslie.ca. I would love to hear your feedback and or your own wondrously eerie bookish tales.

FURTHER READING AND
ADDITIONAL RESOURCES
FOR THE BOOKISH AT HEART

APPENDIX A
Eberhart's List of Haunted Libraries

In October of 2007 and 2008, Senior Editor of *American Libraries*, George M. Eberhart spent the weeks leading up to Halloween posting a comprehensive and compelling daily list of libraries that were reported to be haunted on the Encyclopedia Britannica Blog from across Canada, the United States, and around the world.

As Eberhart writes in one of the summary posts for the lists, "In the fall, a journalist's fancy turns to thoughts of ghosts" and then later jokes that libraries offer "such dynamic mental and sensual stimulation that if haunts are truly evidence for post-mortem survival, I can't imagine anywhere else I'd rather spend my earthly afterlife than in a library."[1]

Eberhart is the author of such fantastic library resource books as *The Whole Library Handbook*, the playful and intriguing *The*

Librarian's Book of Lists as well as *Mysterious Creatures: A Guide to Cryptozoology* (Vols 1 and 2), *The Roswell Report: A Historical Perspective*, and several other books.

Here are links to Eberhart's compiled lists of haunted libraries:

Library Ghosts Canada: *www.britannica.com/blogs/2007/10/ haunted-libraries-in-the-us-utah-wyoming-and-canada/*

Library Ghosts, Northeastern US: *www.britannica.com/ blogs/2008/10/library-ghosts-northeastern-us/*

Library Ghosts, Midwestern US: *www.britannica.com/ blogs/2008/10/library-ghosts-midwestern-us/*

Library Ghosts, Southern US: *www.britannica.com/ blogs/2008/10/library-ghosts-southern-us/*

Library Ghosts, Western US: *www.britannica.com/ blogs/2008/10/library-ghosts-western-us/*

Library Ghosts around the World: www.britannica.com/ blogs/2007/10/haunted-libraries-around-the-world-the-complete-list/

APPENDIX B
Recommended Reading

Books About Books: Fiction

Presented here is a brief list of some fiction titles that feature books as a central topic or theme, or where books, bookstores, or libraries (or those who "haunt" them in the non-scariest of ways), are a main focus of the plot, storyline, or characters.

Bradbury, Ray. *Fahrenheit 451*. New York: Simon & Schuster, 2012.

> In Bradbury's classic novel, firemen exist to burn books, which have been forbidden as a source of despair and unhappiness.

Brenchley, Chaz. *Phantoms at the Phil*. Newcastle, UK: Side Real Press, 2005.

> *Phantoms at the Phil* collects stories set in a library and was derived from an event originally organized by Chaz Brenchley. The event was an opportunity to hear new ghost stories read by their authors in the atmospheric surroundings of Newcastle's private library, the Literary and Philosophical Society. From December 2004 until Twelfth Night 2012, Chaz Brenchley, Gail-Nina Anderson, and Sean O'Brien staged their appearances and readings that inspired the creation of this anthology.

Brooks, Geraldine. *People of the Book*. New York: Viking, 2008.

> An Australian rare-book expert, offered the job of analyzing and conserving a priceless and beautiful book, uncovers a series of tiny artifacts in the ancient binding that leads her to unlock the book's mysteries and explore the book's journey all the way back to its creation.

Campbell, John W. *The Conquest of the Planets* in *Conquest of the Planets & The Man Who Annexed the Moon*. Medford, OR: Armchair Fiction, 2013.

> In a postapocalyptic, postliterate world, an ancient vault filled with books is discovered in the basement of a crumbling building. The rejuvenation of humanity begins with the rediscovery of Earth's past knowledge, preserved by the Interplanetary Library Foundation.

Campbell, Ramsey. *The Overnight*. London: MacMillan, 2006.

> Odd creatures are detected on the security monitors of the bookstore — half-seen beings disappearing behind the stacks — and books are constantly found lying on the floor, broken and water damaged for no good reason. When the staff are called in for an overnight inventory session, the dark evil that has been lurking in the basement unleashes its full terror on the unsuspecting cast of characters.

Cart, Michael. *In the Stacks: Short Stories About Libraries and Librarians*. London: Duckworth Publishers, 2005.

> Librarian Michael Cart has assembled a collection of twentieth century short fiction about libraries and librarians and the love of reading.

Connolly, John. *The Book of Lost Things*. New York: Atria Books, 2006.

> A twelve-year-old boy mourning the loss of his mother has only books to keep him company. As the world around him continues to fall apart, he hears the books whispering to him, and he finds himself pulled into a fantastical world in which a king's secrets are held in a mysterious book.

English, Tom. *Bound for Evil: Curious Tales of Books Gone Bad*. Dead Letter Press. 2008.

> A deluxe illustrated hardcover anthology (limited to 500 copies) that focuses on books. Tom English has collected, sixty-six tales of lost

knowledge and restless ghosts, secret libraries and forbidden texts, including both new and classic tales by dozens of contributors, including Ramsey Campbell, Fred Chappell, H.P. Lovecraft, Jeffrey Thomas, Rhys Hughes, Gary McMahon, M.R. James, and Kurt Newton. This anthology also includes one of my own bookish stories, "Browsers."

Hamilton, Masha. *The Camel Bookmobile*. New York: Harper Perennial, 2007.

Fiona attempts to make her mark by helping to start a travelling library in northeastern Kenya, and becomes caught in a struggle between Western values, modernization, and the traditional ways of an impoverished small community.

Hanff, Helene. *84 Charing Cross Road*. London: Little, Brown Book Group, 2010.

A memoir told through transatlantic letters between a woman in New York and a stodgy bookseller in London; the witty and sarcastic letters blossom into a heart-warming long-distance friendship.

Harris, Charlaine. *Real Murders*. New York: The Berkley Publishing Group, 1990.

Librarian Aurora Teagarden, a member of the Real Murders Club, thinks that meeting once a month to analysis famous crime cases is harmless, until a member of the club is found murdered in exactly the same fashion as a case the group was planning on discussing.

Hoffman, Alice. *The Ice Queen.* **New York: Little, Brown, 2005.**

> A small town librarian is living a normal life until she is struck by lightning, survives, and embarks on a quest to find a man, who, like her, was struck, but with opposite side effects. The two become entwined in a love affair in a story that involves passion, loss, and renewal.

Klages, Ellen. *In the House of the Seven Librarians.* **Seattle: Acqueduct Press, 2012.**

> When an old Carnegie library is closed, its librarians refuse to abandon their home, locking the doors and letting the forest grow around them like a cloak, sheltering them from the rest of the world. But their lives are changed dramatically when a book of fairy tales is found in the book drop, very, very overdue. The payment? A first-born child.

Kostova, Elizabeth. *The Historian.* **New York: Little, Brown, 2005.**

> While exploring her father's library, a young woman discovers an ancient book containing yellowed letters that draws her into dark secrets from her father's past.

Magrs, Paul. *666 Charing Cross Road.* **London: Headline Publishing Group, 2011.**

> An obvious play on the well-known *84 Charing Cross Road* by Helene Hanff, Magrs's story

concerns itself with a battered, leather-bound book stained with vampire blood that arrives in a New York bookshop and somehow brings a mummy to life in a London museum.

Makkai, Rebecca. *The Borrower.* **New York: Viking, 2011.**

A children's librarian attempting to help a young patron escape from an overbearing mother and a pastor's weekly "anti-gay" classes, ends up embarking on a "runaway" road trip from Missouri to Vermont.

Moers, Walter. *The City of Dreaming Books.* **New York: Overlook, 2008.**

Optimus Yarnspinner finds himself stranded in Bookholm, the City of Dreaming Books, where ruthless Bookhunters fight to the death and where he falls into the clutches of an evil genius by the name of Pfistomel Smyke.

Morley, Christopher. *The Haunted Bookshop.* **Fairfiel, IA: 1stWorld Publishing, 2007.**

A charming homage to the world of bookselling, this mysterious tale about unusual happenings at Roger Mifflin's Brooklyn bookshop contains musings about books and publishing that hold up remarkably well even in the modern era.

Morsi, Pamela. *Love Overdue.* **Toronto: Harlequin, 2013.**

Book-loving DJ returns from a spring-break fling to a prim and proper look when she is hired by a rural library. Only, when a mysterious stranger she had her fling with shows up, she finds herself compelled to unpin the bun in her hair and reveal the vixen she had been trying to keep hidden from the world and from herself.

Niffeneggar, Audrey. *The Night Bookmobile*. New York: Abrams, 2010.

The story of a young woman who encounters a mysterious mobile library that happens to stock every book she has ever read.

Peck, Richard. *Here Lies the Librarian*. New York: Dial Books, 2006.

Filled with quirky characters, this humourous novel introduces a young female librarian who turns the lives of a pair of brothers who share a love of classic automobiles upside down.

Powers, Tim. *Salvage and Demolition*. Burton, MI: Subterranean Press, 2013.

A San Francisco-based rare book dealer (Richard Blanzac), opens a box containing consignment items and encounters an unexpected assortment of literary rarities, including a manuscript in verse, an Ace Double Novel, and a scattering of very old cigarette butts. These odd yet commonplace objects serve as catalysts for an extraordinary — and unpredictable — adventure, leading Blanzac from the present day to San Francisco, 1957.

Saintcrow, Lilith. *The Demon's Librarian.* **Memphis, TN: ImaJinn Books, 2009.**

> Librarian Francesca Barnes learns that demons are feeding on the schoolchildren in her city and so digs into the books to research how to best hunt these demons. As she embarks on her quest she learns that she is heir to a long-lost power that might be the key to destroying these demons forever.

Schwab, Victoria. *The Archived.* **New York: Hyperion, 2013.**

> When an otherworldly library called the Archive is compromised from within, a sixteen-year-old named Mackenzie Bishop must prevent violent, ghost-like Histories from escaping into our world.

Setterfield, Diane. *The Thirteenth Tale.* **New York: Atria Books, 2006.**

> On the stairs to her apartment above her father's antiquarian bookshop, biographer Margaret Lea finds a handwritten letter from Vida Winter, one of Britain's most beloved novelists, requesting that Margaret be the one to capture her history. While pondering this task, Margaret begins reading her father's rare copy of Miss Winter's *Thirteen Tales of Change and Desperation*, completely spellbound by the stories, but confused by the fact that there are only twelve stories in the book.

Shulman, Polly. *The Grimm Legacy.* **New York: G.P. Putnam's Sons, 2010.**

> New York high school student Elizabeth gets an after-school job as a page at the "New-York

Circulating Material Repository," a lending library of non-book objects. The job becomes dangerous when magical objects from the Grimm collection are stolen and Elizabeth and the other library pages are drawn into a series of frightening adventures involving mythical creatures.

Sloan, Robin. *Mr. Penumbra's 24-Hour Bookstore*. Toronto: Harper Perennial Canada, 2012.

When Clay Jannon begins working at Mr. Penumbra's 24-Hour Bookstore, he discovers that the strange customers never seem to buy anything and instead "check out" huge obscure volumes from odd corners of the store. When Clay investigates, he learns there are mysteries and secrets that extend far beyond the bookstore's walls.

Wharton, Thomas. *The Logogryph*. Kentville, NS: Gaspereau Press, 2004.

The gift of a suitcase full of old books leads a young man on a lifelong quest for the hidden meaning of books, told as a series of stories about the magic of books and reading.

Wiersema, Robert J. *Bedtime Story*. Toronto: Vintage Canada, 2010.

A novelist reads his son a bedtime story that traps the boy within the fantasy world of the book.

Winkowski, Mary Ann, and Maureen Foley. *The Book of Illumination.* **New York: Three Rivers Press, 2009.**

> A freelance bookbinder who can communicate with ghosts joins forces with Boston's police force and three ghosts to track down a priceless illuminated manuscript stolen from the Boston Athenaeum.

Živković, Zoran. *The Last Book.* **Hornsea, UK: PS Publishers, 2008.**

> A series of mysterious deaths in the Papyrus Bookstore brings literature-loving police inspector Dejan Lukic to investigate. He learns that the only thing the victims have in common is that in the moments before their deaths they were reading an elusive and unidentified volume called *The Last Book*.

Živković, Zoran. *The Library.* **Chuo-ku, Japan: Kurodahan Press, 2010.**

> A cycle of six thematically linked stories, droll renditions of the nightmares ensuing upon misplaced, or (of course) excessive, bibliophilia. A writer encounters a website where all his possible future books are on display; a lonely man faces an infinite flow of hardback books through his mailbox; an ordinary library turns by night into an archive of souls; the Devil sets about raising standards of infernal literacy; one book houses all books; a connoisseur of hardcovers strives to expel a lone paperback from his collection.

Zusak, Markus. *The Book Thief*. New York: Alfred A. Knopf, 2005.

> A foster girl living outside Munich in Nazi Germany who is making her living stealing learns to read and to share her stolen books with her neighbours during the bombing raids.

Series (Information for the first book in the series is provided)

Dunning, John. *Booked to Die*. New York: Simon & Schuster, 2012.

> Cliff Janeway Series: *Booked To Die, The Bookman's Wake, The Bookman's Promise, The Sign of the Book, The Bookwoman's Last Fling*

> Cliff Janeway, a cop and rare book expert in Denver, Colorado, doesn't always play by the book in this mystery series.

Fforde, Jasper. *The Eyre Affair*. London: Hodder and Stoughton, 2001.

> Thursday Next Series: *The Eyre Affair, Lost in a Good Book, The Well of Lost Plots, Something Rotton, First Among Sequels, One of Our Thursdays is Missing, The Woman Who Died a Lot, Dark Reading Matter*

> Thursday Next is a literary detective who goes inside books from her futuristic time-travel world.

Appendix B

Funke, Cornelia. *Inkheart*. New York: Scholastic, 2003.

Inkworld Series: *Inkheart, Inkspell, Inkdeath*

Twelve-year-old Meggie learns that her father, who repairs books for a living, can bring fictional characters to life merely by reading them. But some of the characters can exact evil and trap humans in their fictional kingdom.

Glennon, Paul. *Bookweird*. Toronto: Doubleday Canada, 2008.

Bookweird Sereis: *Bookweird, Bookweirder, Bookweirdest*

An eleven-year-old kid, who absentmindedly begins nibbling on the edge of a page, finds himself waking up inside the book he was chewing on. Norman learns of a special hidden power and the mysterious force known as "Bookweird" that propels him through the book in a way that he can also mess up the story's proper plotlines.

Harper, Molly. *Nice Girls Don't Have Fangs*. New York: Pocket Star Books, 2009. Jane Jameson (Series), Molly Harper

Jane Jameson Series: *Nice Girls Don't Have Fangs, Nice Girls Don't Date Dead Men, Nice Girls Don't Live Forever, Nice Girls Don't Sign a Lease Without a Wedding Ring, Nice Girls Don't Bite Their Neighbors*

Children's librarian and self-professed nice girl Jane Jameson is accidentally shot by a hunter and left for dead — but she is rescued by a mysterious

243

stranger who, in order to save her, converts her into a vampire. What's a nice undead girl to do?

Hines, Jim C. *Libromancer*. New York: Penguin, 2012.

Magic Ex Libris Series: *Libromancer, Codex Born*

Libriomancers are gifted with the ability to magically reach into books and draw forth objects. Isaac Vainio is a Libriomancer, a member of the secret organization founded five centuries ago by Johannes Gutenberg, and the main hero in this series.

James, Miranda. *Murder Past Due*. New York: The Berkley Publishing Group, 2010.

Cat in the Stacks Mysteries: *Murder Past Due, Classified as Murder, File M for Murder, Out of Circulation, The Silence of the Library*

Charlie Harris, a widowed librarian, and Diesel, her Maine Coon cat, pair up to solve crimes in the college town of Athena, Mississippi.

Kelly, Sofie. *Curiosity Thrilled the Cat*. New York: Obsidian, 2011.

Magical Cats Mystery Series: *Curiosity Thrilled the Cat, Sleight of Paws, Copycat Killing, Cat Trick, Final Catcall, A Midwinter's Tail*

Kathleen Paulson, a librarian from Boston, and two stray cats with special powers, Owen and Hercules, solve crimes in fictional Mayville Heights, Minnesota.

Kimberly, Alice. *The Ghost and Mrs. McClure*. New York: The Berkley Publishing Group, 2004.

> Haunted Bookshop Mystery Series: *The Ghost and Mrs. McClure, The Ghost and the Dead Deb, The Ghost and the Dead Man's Library, The Ghost and the Femme Fatale, The Ghost and the Haunted Mansion, The Ghost and the Bogus Bookseller*

> Penelope Thornton-McClure, a bookshop owner who manages a bookshop that is haunted, teams up with the store's resident ghost-sleuth, Jack Shepard, in Quindicott, Rhode Island, to solve local bookish mysteries.

McKinlay, Jenn. *Books Can Be Deceiving*. New York: The Berkley Publishing Group, 2011.

> Library Lover's Mystery Series: *Books Can Be Deceiving, Due or Die, Book, Line and Sinker, Read It and Weep, On Borrowed Time*

> Lindsay Norris, Director of the Brier Creek Public Library in Connecticut, finds herself in situations where she has to unravel and solve local mysteries.

Odom, Mel. *The Rover*. New York: Tor, 2002.

> The Rover Series: *The Rover, The Destruction of the Books, Lord of the Libraries, The Quest for the Trilogy*

Edgewick Lamplighter ("Wick," to his friends) is a humble librarian in the isolated halls of Greydawn Moors until dreams of wanderlust and a bit of dereliction in his duties result in his being shanghaied to a far-off land.

Zafon, Carlos Ruiz. *The Shadow of the Wind*. New York: Penguin, 2001.

> The Cemetery of Forgotten Books Series: *The Shadow of the Wind, The Angel's Game, The Rose of Fire, The Prisoner of Heaven*

> Hidden in the heart of the city of Barcelona is the "cemetery of lost books" — a labyrinth library of obscure and forgotten titles that have long gone out of print.

Graphic Novels & Comics About Books

Anbaum, Gene and Bill Barnes. *Unshelved*. Overdue Media.

> *Unshelved* is the world's only daily comic strip set in a public library and written by a real-life librarian, including some stories that are made up, others that are based on real life, and stories sent in from readers.

Turner, James. *Rex Libris*. v 1–13. San Jose, CA: Salve Labor Graphics.

> Rex Libris, Head Librarian at Middleton Public Library, fights in an unending struggle against the forces of ignorance and darkness, travelling to the farthest reaches of the galaxy in search of overdue books. Wearing super thick pop bottle glasses and armed with an arsenal of high technology weapons, he strikes fear into recalcitrant borrowers, and can take on virtually any foe, from zombies to renegade literary characters.

Yumi, Kiiro and Arikawa, Hiro. *Library Wars: Love & War*. v. 1-13. Tokyo, Japan: MediaWorks.

> In the near future, the federal government creates a committee to rid society of books it deems unsuitable. The libraries vow to protect their collections, and with the help of local governments, form a military group to defend themselves — the Library Forces!

Spooky Reading

Balzano, Christopher and Tim Weisberg. *Haunted Objects: Stories of Ghosts on your Shelf*. Iola, KS: Krause Publications, 2012.

Barrett, William F. *On The Threshold of the Unseen*. New York: E.P. Dutton & Company, 1918.

Brown, Alan. *Haunted Meridian, Mississippi*. Charleston: The Haunted Press, 2011.

Colombo, John Robert. *Ghost Stories of Canada*. Toronto: Dundurn, 2000.

Colombo, John Robert. *Haunted Toronto*. Toronto: Dundurn, 1996.

Cook, Rita. *Haunted Fort Worth*. Charleston: The History Press, 2011.

Coulombe, Charles A. *Haunted Castles of the World*. New York: Globe Pequot Press, 2004.

Diel, Daniel and Mark Donnelly. *Haunted Houses: Guide to Spooky, Creepy and Strange Places Across the USA*.

Mechanicsburg, PA: Stackpole Books, 2010.

Dunne, John. *A Ghost Watcher's Guide to Ireland*. Louisiana: Appletree Press, 2001.

Eberhart, George M. *The Whole Library Handbook 4*. New York: American Library Association, 2006.

Guiley, Rosemary Ellen. *Encyclopedia of Ghosts and Spirits*. New York: Facts on File, Inc., 1992.

Hladik, Laura. *Ghosthunting New Jersey*. Cincinnati, OH: Clerisy Press, 2008.

Jenkins, Greg. *Florida's Ghostly Legends and Haunted Folklore: The Gulf Coast and Pensacola*. Sarasota, FL: Pineapple Press, 2007.

Karl, Jason. *An Illustrated History of the Haunted World*. London: New Holland Publishers, 2007.

Leslie, Mark. *Haunted Hamilton: The Ghosts of Dundurn Castle and Other Steeltown Shivers*. Toronto: Dundurn, 2012.

Leslie, Mark and Jenny Jelen. *Spooky Sudbury: True Tales of the Eerie & Unexplained*. Toronto: Dundurn, 2013.

Martinelli, Patricia A. and Charles A. Stansfield, Jr. *The Big Book of New Jersey Ghost Stories*. Mechanicsburg, PA: Stackpole Books, 2013.

McCarthy, Stephanie E. *Haunted Peoria*. Chicago: Arcadia Publishing, 2009.

Newman, Rich. *The Ghost Hunters Field Guide*. Woodbury, MN: Llewellyn, 2011.

Penot, Jessica. *Haunted North Alabama*. Charleston: The History Press, 2010.

Slaughter, April. *Ghosthunting Texas*. Cincinnati, OH: Clerisy Press, 2009.

Smith, Barbara. *Ghost Stories of Alberta*. Toronto: Dundurn, 1993.

Smyth, Richard. *Bloody British History: Leeds*. Stroud, UK: The History Press, 2013.

Stam, David H. *International Dictionary of Library Histories*. Chicago: Fitzroy Dearborn Publishers, 2001.

Taylor, Troy. *Haunted Illinois: Ghosts and Strange Phenomenon of the Prairie State*. Mechanicsburg, PA: Stackpole Books, 2008.

Vernon, Steve. *Halifax Haunts: Exploring the City's Spookiest Spaces*. Halifax, NS: Nimbus Publishing, 2009.

Weisberg, Tim. *Ghosts of the SouthCoast*. Charleston: The History Press, 2008.

Whitington, Mitchel. *Ghosts of North Texas*. Lanham, MD: Rowman & Littlefield Publishing Group, 2003.

Winn, Christopher. *Things I Never Knew About the Scottish*. London, Ebury Publishing, 2009.

APPENDIX C
Bookseller Associations

What follows is a very brief list of some of the larger book-seller associations around the world. These types of associations offer independently run businesses the opportunity to unite in unique and valuable ways, not just for advocacy but for collaborative tool-building, networking, and mutual support. But most importantly, these association websites very often provide lists of their member stores making it easy for you to find a great local bookstore near your community.

American Bookseller's Association: *www.bookweb.org/*

Antiquarian Booksellers' Association of Canada: *www.abac.org/ home.php*

Australian Booksellers Association: *www.aba.org.au/*

The Booksellers Association (UK): *www.booksellers.org.uk/*

Booksellers New Zealand: *www.booksellers.co.nz/*

Campus Retail Canada: *www.campusretail.com/*

Campus Stores Canada: *www.campusstores.ca/*

Canadian Booksellers Association: *www.retailcouncil.org/mystore/booksellers*

European and International Bookseller's Federation: *http://eibf-booksellers.org/*

Independent College Bookstore Association: *http://www.icbainc.com/*

Independent Online Booksellers Association: *www.ioba.org/pages/*

NOTES

Canada

1. Barbara Smith, *Ghost Stories of Alberta* (Toronto: Dundurn, 1993), 23.
2. Ibid.
3. Barbara Smith, *Ghost Stories of Alberta* (Toronto: Dundurn, 1993), 24.
4. Ibid.
5. Ibid.
6. Ibid.
7. Ibid.
8. Barbara Smith, *Ghost Stories of Alberta* (Toronto: Dundurn, 1993), 23.
9. Mark Leslie, *Haunted Hamilton: The Ghosts of Dundurn Castle & Other Steeltown Shivers.* (Dundurn: Toronto), 116.
10. "Waterdown Branch," Hamilton Public Library, *http://www.hpl. ca/branches/waterdown-branch.*
11. Ibid.
12. Ibid.
13. "Is There Really A Ghost Hitchhiker That Haunts UBC 'University Boulevard'?," *604 Now, http://604now. com/2011/10/is-there-really-a-ghost-hitchhiker-that-haunts-ubc-university-boulevard/.*
14. Mary Frances Hill, "Our favourite haunts: Some of Vancouver's oldest residents

just can't say goodbye," *http://
www.vancouversun.com/
news/vancouver-125/favour-
ite+haunts/4523225/story.html.*

15. Ibid.

16. PSICAN, "Ghosts of UBC," *http://
www.psican.org/alpha/index.php?/
British-Columbia-Ghost-Reports/
Ghosts-Of-UBC.html.*

17. Andrea Coutts, "Explore the
haunted and unusual this
Halloween," October 31,
2013, *http://about.library.ubc.
ca/2013/10/31/explore-the-
haunted-and-unusual-this-
halloween/.*

18. Ibid.

19. John Robert Colombo, *Ghost
Stories of Canada* (Toronto:
Dundurn, 2000), 108.

20. Ibid.

21. Ibid.

22. Ibid.

23. Ibid.

24. Ibid.

25. "Runnymede Theatre,"
*Wikipedia, http://en.wikipedia.
org/wiki/Runnymede_Theatre.*

26. "Runnymede Theatre,"
The Toronto and Ontario
Ghosts and Hauntings
Research Society, *http://
www.torontoghosts.org/index.
php?/20080815140/The-Former-
City-Of-Toronto-Private-
Business/Runnymede-Theatre/
All-Pages.html.*

27. Ibid.

28. Ibid.

29. Kate Fane, "Ghost City: The
Runnymede Theatre," *The Grid*,
November 14, 2013, *http://
www.thegridto.com/city/places/*

ghost-city-the-runnymede-
theatre/.*

30. Ibid.

31. Ibid.

32. Emily Temple, "Readers'
Choice: 20 More Beautiful
Bookstores from Around the
World," *Flavorwire*, February
28, 2012, *http://flavorwire.
com/264130/readers-choice-20-
more-beautiful-bookstores-from-
around-the-world#6.*

33. Marc Weisblott, "Big box
bookstore that faced a protest
for opening now being
protested for closing," *Canada.
com*, January 28, 2013, *http://o.
canada.com/business/chapters-
runnymede-theatre-closing/.*

34. Ibid.

35. Francine Kopoun, "Runnymede
Chapters closing, with Shoppers
Drug Mart moving into
heritage premises," *Toronto Star*,
November 7, 2013, *http://www.
thestar.com/business/2013/11/07/
runnymede_chapters_closing_
with_shoppers_drug_mart_
moving_into_heritage_premises.
html.*

36. Mary Baxter, "Haunted
London: Attic Books," *London
Community News*, October 25,
2012.

37. Ibid.

38. Ibid.

39. Ibid.

40. Ibid.

41. Ibid.

42. Ibid.

43. "Attic Books," *Wikipedia,
http://en.wikipedia.org/wiki/
Attic_Books.*

44. "About Us," Attic Books, *http:// www.atticbooks.ca/aboutus.html*.

45. Steve Vernon, *Halifax Haunts: Exploring the City's Spookiest Spaces* (Halifax: Nimbus Publishing, 2009), 73.

46. Ibid, 69–71.

47. Ibid, 71.

48. Ibid, 70.

49. Ibid, 71.

50. Ibid.

51. Ibid, 68.

52. Ibid, 73.

53. "Spring Garden Road — 50th Anniversary," Halifax Public Libraries, *http://www. halifaxpubliclibraries.ca/research/ topics/local-history-genealogy/ sgr-50.html*.

54. Ibid.

55. "Village Library," The Society for the Preservation of Historic Thornhill, *http://www. thornhillhistoric.org/walktour_ slide1.html*.

56. Pearson Bowerman, "Historic Library Remains," *Toronto Star*, January 12, 1988.

57. Ibid.

58. Ibid.

59. Ibid.

60. Ibid.

61. Deborah Smith, "Who is Haunting the Village Library?"

62. Ibid.

63. Kevin Stevenson, "Spooky Spirit Along Library Patrons."

64. Ibid.

65. Deborah Smith, "Who is Haunting the Village Library?"

66. Kevin Stevenson, "Spooky Spirit Along Library Patrons."

67. Deborah Smith, "Who is Haunting the Village Library?"

68. Ibid.

69. Kevin Stevenson, "Spooky Spirit Along Library Patrons."

70. Ibid.

71. Lance Holdforth, "World War I book acts as catalyst for local man," *Barrie Examiner*, October 30, 2012, *http:// www.thebarrieexaminer. com/2012/10/30/world-war-i-book-acts-as-catalyst-for-local-man*.

72. Ibid.

73. Ibid.

74. Ibid.

75. Ibid.

76. Ibid.

77. Ibid.

78. Ibid.

79. Ibid.

80. Ibid.

81. Ibid.

82. Ibid.

83. Lance Holdforth, "TV's Ghost Girls tackle popular Barrie book store," *Barrie Examiner*, October 30, 2012, *http://www.thebarrieexaminer. com/2012/10/30/tvs-ghost-girls-tackle-popular-barrie-bookstore*.

84. Ibid.

85. Ibid.

86. John Robert Colombo, *Haunted Toronto* (Toronto: Dundurn, 1996), 97.

87. Ibid, 97–98.

88. John Robert Colombo, *Mysteries of Ontario* (Toronto: Dundurn, 1999), 228.

89. Ibid, 229.

90. Ibid, 228.
91. "Algernon Blackwood," *Wikipedia, http://en.wikipedia. org/wiki/Algernon_Blackwood.*
92. "Supernatural Horror in Literature," *Wikipedia, http://en.wikipedia.org/wiki/ Supernatural_Horror_in_ Literature.*
93. "History of the Grange," Art Gallery of Ontario, *http://www. ago.net/history-of-the-grange.*
94. Ibid.
95. Ibid.
96. "Our Mandate," Art Gallery of Ontario, *http://www.ago.net/ mandate.*
97. "About Rare Books and Special Collections," McGill Library, *https://www.mcgill.ca/library/ branches/rarebooks/about.*
98. Tim Hornyak, "Is there a spectre in the stacks?," *McGill News Alumni Magazine, http://publications.mcgill.ca/ mcgillnews/2012/10/26/is-there- a-specter-in-the-stacks/.*
99. Ibid.
100. Matt Herzfeld, "John Wilkes Booth lived here," *McGill Daily,* January 26, 2012.
101. "About the Collection," Lincoln North, *http://digital.library. mcgill.ca/lincoln/cover.htm.*
102. Kyla Mandel, "Haunted McGill," *McGill Tribune,* October 24, 2011.
103. "About the library," McGill Library, *https://www.mcgill.ca/ library/about.*
104. "McLennan Library Building," Virtual McGill, *http://cac.mcgill. ca/campus/buildings/McLennan_ Library.html.*
105. "About Rare Books and Special Collections," McGill Library, *https://www.mcgill.ca/library/ branches/rarebooks/about.*
106. "The Fire of 1916," Public Works and Government Services Canada, *http:// www.tpsgc-pwgsc.gc.ca/ collineduparlement- parliamenthill/batir-building/ hist/1916-eng.html.*
107. "1916: Fire destroys Parliamentary Buildings," CBC Digital Archives, *http:// www.cbc.ca/archives/categories/ politics/federal-politics/fire- destroys-parliament-buildings. html.*
108. "The Fire of 1916," Public Works and Government Services Canada, *http:// www.tpsgc-pwgsc.gc.ca/ collineduparlement- parliamenthill/batir-building/ hist/1916-eng.html.*
109. Ibid.
110. "1916: Fire destroys Parliamentary Buildings," CBC Digital Archives, *http:// www.cbc.ca/archives/categories/ politics/federal-politics/fire- destroys-parliament-buildings. html.*
111. "The Fire of 1916," Public Works and Government Services Canada, http:// *www.tpsgc-pwgsc.gc.ca/ collineduparlement- parliamenthill/batir-building/ hist/1916-eng.html.*
112. "The Library of Parliament," Parliament of Canada, *http://www.parl.gc.ca/About/ Parliament/Publications/LOP/*

lop-e.asp.

113. Ibid.

114. "The Library of Parliament," *Wikipedia, http://www.parl. gc.ca/About/Parliament/ Publications/LOP/lop-e.asp.*

115. Ibid.

United States of America

1. Amanda Festa, "Finding Jack Kerouac in St. Petersburg, Florida," *Literary Traveler* (blog), March 22, 2013, *http:// www.literarytraveler.net/ blog/2013/03/finding-jack-kerouac-in-st-petersburg-florida/.*

2. Anastasia Dawson, "Haslam's Book Store in St Pete celebrates 80 years," *St Petersburg Tribune,* December 8, 2013.

3. "Haslam's Book Store," *Ghost Report, http://www. ghostreport.com/states/florida/ HaslamsBookstore.htm.*

4. Laura Kadechka, "Haslam's Bookstore survives mega stores, racing against e-book revolution," *10 News,* February 15, 2011, *http://origin.tampabays10. com/money/costing/story. aspx?storyid=175126.*

5. Greg Jenkins, *Florida's Ghostly Legends and Haunted Folklore: The Gulf Coast and Pensacola* (Sarasota, FL: Pineapple Press, 2007), 131–32.

6. Ibid.

7. Anastasia Dawson, "Haslam's Book Store in St Pete celebrates 80 years," *St Petersburg Tribune,* December 8, 2013.

8. Ibid.

9. Laura Kadechka, "Haslam's Bookstore survives mega stores, racing against e-book revolution," *10 News,* February 15, 2011, *http://origin.tampabays10. com/money/costing/story. aspx?storyid=175126.*

10. Greg Jenkins, *Florida's Ghostly Legends and Haunted Folklore: The Gulf Coast and Pensacola* (Sarasota, FL: Pineapple Press, 2007), 133.

11. Ibid.

12. Greg Jenkins, *Florida's Ghostly Legends and Haunted Folklore: The Gulf Coast and Pensacola* (Sarasota, FL: Pineapple Press, 2007), 132.

13. Tom Zucco, "Hunts for Haunts," *St. Petersburg Times,* October 31, 2002.

14. "Charles Haslam Dies at 70," *St Petersburg Times,* October 11, 1983.

15. Anastasia Dawson, "Haslam's Book Store in St Pete celebrates 80 years," *St Petersburg Tribune,* December 8, 2013.

16. "The Haslam Family & Their Bookstore," Haslam's, *http:// www.haslams.com/history.shtml.*

17. "Haslam's Book Store," *Ghost Report, http://www. ghostreport.com/states/florida/ HaslamsBookstore.htm.*

18. Jessica Penot, *Haunted North Alabama* (Charleston: The History Press, 2010).

19. AD Spencer, "Ghosts and Campus Hauntings: The University of North Alabama

in Florence, Alabama," *Yahoo Voices, http://voices.yahoo. com/ghosts-campus-hauntings-university-north-4516979. html?cat=8.*

20. Jessica Penot, *Haunted North Alabama* (Charleston: The History Press, 2010).
21. Ibid.
22. Ibid.
23. Ibid.
24. Ibid.
25. Ibid.
26. AD Spencer, "Ghosts and Campus Hauntings: The University of North Alabama in Florence, Alabama," *Yahoo Voices, http://voices.yahoo. com/ghosts-campus-hauntings-university-north-4516979. html?cat=8.*
27. Ibid.
28. Jessica Penot, *Haunted North Alabama* (Charleston: The History Press, 2010).
29. Ibid.
30. "The Lady of the Lake (Poem)," *Wikipedia, http://en.wikipedia. org/wiki/The_Lady_of_the_ Lake_%28poem%29.*
31. "The Hauntings of the Seven Sisters Inn," Seven Sisters Inn, *http://sevensistersinnhauntings. webs.com/.*
32. Christopher Balzano and Tim Weisberg, *Haunted Objects: Stories of Ghosts on your Shelf,* (Iola, KS: Krause Publications, 2012), 68–69.
33. Ibid, 69–70.
34. Ibid, 70.
35. Ibid.

36. Ibid.
37. Ibid, 70–71.
38. Ibid, 71.
39. Ibid, 71–72.
40. Ibid, 72.
41. Ibid.
42. Ibid.
43. "Working With Ghosts — A Haunted Bookstore," *Biblioblog* (blog), October 2, 2007, *http:// www.biblio.com/blog/2007/10/ haunted-bookstore/.*
44. Ibid.
45. Ibid.
46. Ibid.
47. "About us," The Book House, *http://www.bookhousestl. com/?page=shop/aboutus.*
48. Ibid.
49. Claire Kirch, "Book House Issues Call to Stave Off Eviction," *Publisher's Weekly,* April 29, 2013, *http://www. publishersweekly.com/pw/by-topic/industry-news/bookselling/ article/57010-book-house-issues-call-threatened-with-eviction. html.*
50. Steve Giegerich, "The Book House, a Rock Hill Institution is forced to close," *St. Louis Post Dispatch,* May 1, 2013, *http:// www.stltoday.com/news/local/ metro/the-book-house-a-rock-hill-institution-is-forced-to/ article_31c51b2d-56f6-579d-a8aa-78efd474c0ec.html.*
51. Lindsay Toler, "As Construction Costs Mount, Book House Owner Michelle Baron Launches Kickstarter," *Daily Riverfront Times,* November 12, 2013, *http://blogs.riverfronttimes.*

com/dailyrft/2013/11/as_
construction_costs_mount_book_
house_black_friday.php.

52. "Help Build the Book
House!," Kickstarter, https://
www.kickstarter.com/
projects/1338431583/help-build-
the-book-house.

53. Doug Miner, "The Book House,
Freeman Marketing cut the
ribbon," *40 South News*, March
19, 2014, http://40southnews.
com/the-book-house-owner-cuts-
the-ribbon/.

54. Jane Henderson, "Book House
says it is open in Maplewood,"
St. Louis Post Dispatch,
February 12, 2014, http://www.
stltoday.com/entertainment/
books-and-literature/book-blog/
book-house-says-it-is-open-in-
maplewood/article_78e5331a-
fff2-5d15-ac52-eebf40071f1a.
html.

55. "'Haunted Collector': In a
Haunted Bookstore, A Child's
Ghost Speaks And Moves Toys,"
Huffington Post, July 19, 2012,
http://www.huffingtonpost.
com/2012/07/19/haunted-
collector-child-ghost-speaks-
moves-toys-video_n_1685322.
html.

56. "Haunted Browse Awhile
Books," *Facebook*, https://www.
facebook.com/pages/Haunted-
Browse-Awhile-Books/22128607
4582498?id=221286074582498
&sk=info.

57. Ibid.

58. Ibid.

59. Ibid.

60. DIGS Paranormal Videos,

Movies, and horror reviews,
"Haunted Browse Awhile
Books: Part 1: Walkthrough:
Meeting one with ghost Erika,"
YouTube (video), April 15,
2012, https://www.youtube.com/
watch?v=bkrDStF81aU.

61. ParanormalAnswers, "Browse
Awhile Books Part 3 of
3 — Paranormal Answers
Research Team," YouTube
(video), January 13, 2013,
https://www.youtube.com/
watch?v=1c0WyDXft1Q.

62. "Haunted Browse Awhile
Books," *Facebook*, https://www.
facebook.com/pages/Haunted-
Browse-Awhile-Books/22128607
4582498?id=221286074582498
&sk=info.

63. "Barber's Book Store,"
Architecture in Fort Worth,
http://www.fortwortharchitecture.
com/barbers.htm.

64. Mitchel Whitington, *Ghosts
of North Texas* (Lanham,
MD: Rowman & Littlefield
Publishing Group, 2003), 104.

65. Rita Cook, *Haunted Fort Worth*
(Charleston: The History Press,
2011), 66.

66. Mitchel Whitington, *Ghosts
of North Texas* (Lanham,
MD: Rowman & Littlefield
Publishing Group, 2003), 104.

67. Rita Cook, *Haunted Fort Worth*
(Charleston: The History Press,
2011), 66.

68. Mitchel Whitington, *Ghosts
of North Texas* (Lanham,
MD: Rowman & Littlefield
Publishing Group, 2003),
104–105.

69. "Barber's Book Store," *Architecture in Fort Worth*, *http://www.fortwortharchitecture. com/barbers.htm.*

70. Rita Cook, *Haunted Fort Worth* (Charleston: The History Press, 2011), 66.

71. "Mary Reed Hall," *Wikipedia*, *http://en.wikipedia.org/wiki/ Mary_Reed_Hall.*

72. "DU Campus," University of Denver, *http://www.du.edu/ explore/campus/index.html.*

73. Charles Ng, "Mary Reed ghost story," *Clarion*, October 30, 2003, *http://duclarion.com/ mary-reed-ghost-story-4/.*

74. "Mary Reed Hall," *Wikipedia*, *http://en.wikipedia.org/wiki/ Mary_Reed_Hall.*

75. Charles Ng, "Mary Reed ghost story," *Clarion*, October 30, 2003, *http://duclarion.com/ mary-reed-ghost-story-4/.*

76. Ibid.

77. "Biographical Sketch of Marcella Miller Du Pont," Penrose Library, *http://lib-anubis.cair.du.edu/About/ collections/SpecialCollections/ Miller-duPont/marcellabio.cfm.*

78. "Beware, the ghost of Mary Reed lurks…," *Clarion*, October 29, 2007, *http://duclarion.com/ beware-the-ghost-of-mary-reed-lurks-3/.*

79. Ibid.

80. "Mary Reed Hall," *Wikipedia*, http://en.wikipedia.org/wiki/ Mary_Reed_Hall.

81. "Beware, the ghost of Mary Reed lurks…," *Clarion*, October 29, 2007, *http://duclarion.com/ beware-the-ghost-of-mary-reed-lurks-3/.*

82. Ibid.

83. "The Natatorium," *Haunted Houses*, *http://www. hauntedhouses.com/states/tx/ natatorium.htm.*

84. "Amarillo Natatorium," Texas Historical Commission, *http:// atlas.thc.state.tx.us/shell-kword. htm.*

85. April Slaughter, *Ghosthunting Texas* (Cincinnati, OH: Clerisy Press, 2009), 7.

86. "The Natatorium," *Haunted Houses*, http://www. hauntedhouses.com/states/tx/ natatorium.htm.

87. April Slaughter, *Ghosthunting Texas* (Cincinnati, OH: Clerisy Press, 2009), 8.

88. Ibid.

89. April Slaughter, *Ghosthunting Texas* (Cincinnati, OH: Clerisy Press, 2009), 9.

90. Ibid.

91. April Slaughter, *Ghosthunting Texas* (Cincinnati, OH: Clerisy Press, 2009), 10–11.

92. "Godfrey Campus History," Lewis & Clark Community College, *http://www.lc.edu/ Godfrey-history/.*

93. Troy Taylor, *Haunted Illinois: Ghosts and Strange Phenomenon of the Prairie State* (Mechanicsburg, PA: Stackpole Books, 2008), 42.

94. Troy Taylor, *Haunted Illinois: Ghosts and Strange Phenomenon of the Prairie State* (Mechanicsburg, PA: Stackpole Books, 2008), 44.

95. Ibid.

96. Troy Taylor, "Ghost Stories from Haunted Alton: The Ghost of Harriet Haskell," Alton Hauntings, *http://www.altonhauntings.com/lewisclark.html.*

97. Ibid.

98. Ibid.

99. Ibid.

100. Ibid.

101. "Godfrey Campus History," Lewis & Clark Community College, *http://www.lc.edu/Godfrey-history/.*

102. Troy Taylor, *Haunted Illinois: Ghosts and Strange Phenomenon of the Prairie State* (Mechanicsburg, PA: Stackpole Books, 2008), 42

103. "Godfrey Campus History," Lewis & Clark Community College, *http://www.lc.edu/Godfrey-history/.*

104. Ibid.

105. Troy Taylor, *Haunted Illinois: Ghosts and Strange Phenomenon of the Prairie State* (Mechanicsburg, PA: Stackpole Books, 2008), 42.

106. Troy Taylor, "Ghost Stories from Haunted Alton: The Ghost of Harriet Haskell," Alton Hauntings, *http://www.altonhauntings.com/lewisclark.html.*

107. Ibid.

108. Troy Taylor, *Haunted Illinois: Ghosts and Strange Phenomenon of the Prairie State* (Mechanicsburg, PA: Stackpole Books, 2008), 43.

109. Ibid.

110. Troy Taylor, "Ghost Stories from Haunted Alton: The Ghost of Harriet Haskell," Alton Hauntings, *http://www.altonhauntings.com/lewisclark.html.*

111. Emily Gilmore Alden, *Harriet Newell Haskell: A Span of Sunshine Gold,* (Boston: s.n., 1908), 10–11.

112. Mark Constantino and Debby Constantino, "Spellbinding Tales Bookstore Investigation," Spirits-Speak, *http://www.spirits-speak.com/investigations_spellbinding.html.*

113. "Spellbinding Tales: A Haunted Bookstore Gives Us A Learning Experience!," Ghost Trackers, 2010, *http://www.ghost-trackers.org/spellbinding.htm.*

114. Ibid.

115. Mark Constantino and Debby Constantino, "Spellbinding Tales Bookstore Investigation," Spirits-Speak, *http://www.spirits-speak.com/investigations_spellbinding.html.*

116. Ibid.

117. Ibid.

118. "Spellbinding Tales: A Haunted Bookstore Gives Us A Learning Experience!," Ghost Trackers, 2010, *http://www.ghost-trackers.org/spellbinding.htm.*

119. Janet Levaux, "A spirited look at Alameda hauntings," *San Jose Mercury News*, September 30, 2008, *http://www.mercurynews.com/alamedacounty/ci_10858892.*

120. "Carnegie Library (Parkersburg, West

Virginia)," *Wikipedia, http://
en.wikipedia.org/wiki/Carnegie_
Library_%28Parkersburg,_West_
Virginia%29.*

121. "Andrew Carnegie," *Wikipedia,
http://en.wikipedia.org/wiki/
Andrew_Carnegie.*

122. Larry Brian Radka, "The Old
Parkersburg Carnegie Public
Library," *History Inside Pictures,
http://www.historyinsidepictures.
com/Pages/TheOldParkersburg-
CarnegiePublicLibrary.aspx.*

123. Ibid.

124. Ibid.

125. "Haunted Bookstore," Trans-
Allegheny Bookstore, *http://
users.wirefire.com/magick/
new_page_18.htm.*

126. Ibid.

127. Theresa Racer, "Trans-
Allegheny Bookstore,
Parkersburg," *Theresa's
Haunted History of the Tri-State*
(blog), May 23, 2011, *http://
theresashauntedhistoryofthetri-
state.blogspot.com/2011/05/
trans-allegheny-bookstore-
parkersburg.html.*

128. Ibid.

129. Ibid.

130. Ibid.

131. Justin D. Anderson, "31 women
are serving life in prison in
state," *Times West Virginia,*
August 19, 2007, *http://www.
timeswv.com/westvirginia/
x681654656/31-women-are-
serving-life-in-prison-in-state.*

132. Theresa Racer, "Trans-
Allegheny Bookstore,
Parkersburg," *Theresa's
Haunted History of the Tri-State*

(blog), May 23, 2011, *http://
theresashauntedhistoryofthetri-
state.blogspot.com/2011/05/
trans-allegheny-bookstore-
parkersburg.html.*

133. Jess Mancini, "Trans Allegheny
Books closing," *Marietta
Times,* October 6, 2010, *http://
www.mariettatimes.com/page/
content.detail/id/530384/
Trans-Allegheny-Books-closing.
html?nav=5002.*

134. Natalie Seely, "Injunction
prohibits sale of Trans
Allegheny," *Parkersburg News
and Sentinel,* April 1, 2011,
*https://www.newsandsentinel.
com/page/content.detail/
id/546367/Injunction-prohibits-
sale-of-Trans-Allegheny.
html?nav=5061.*

135. "The Grey Lady of Willard
Library," Willard Library, *http://
www.willard.lib.in.us/about_
willard_library/Grey-Lady.pdf.*

136. Ibid.

137. Mark Merimen, Troy Taylor,
and James A. Willis, *Weird
Indiana* (New York: Sterling
Publishing), 184.

138. Ibid.

139. Ibid.

140. Mark Merimen, Troy Taylor,
and James A. Willis, *Weird
Indiana* (New York: Sterling
Publishing), 185.

141. Willard Library, "The Grey
Lady of Willard Library," *http://
www.willard.lib.in.us/about_
willard_library/Grey-Lady.pdf.*

142. Ibid.

143. Ibid.

144. Ibid.
145. Ibid.
146. "A Timeline of Willard Library," Willard Library, http://www.willard.lib.in.us/about_willard_library/history/a_timeline_of_willard_library.php.
147. "About Willard Library — History," Willard Library, http://www.willard.lib.in.us/about_willard_library/history.php.
148. "The Grey Lady of Willard Library," Willard Library, http://www.willard.lib.in.us/about_willard_library/Grey-Lady.pdf.
149. "About Willard Library — History," Willard Library, http://www.willard.lib.in.us/about_willard_library/history.php.
150. Ibid.
151. Ibid.
152. Ibid.
153. Ibid.
154. "The Lady in Grey," Willard Ghost, Willard Library, http://www.willardghost.com/.
155. Ibid.
156. "Speaking Ill of the Dead?," Willard Library, http://www.willard.lib.in.us/about_willard_library/history/speaking_ill_of_the_dead.php.
157. "Who is the Ghost?," Willard Ghost, Willard Library, http://www.willardghost.com/index.php?content=whoistheghost.
158. "About Peace of Mind Books," Peace of Mind Books, http://pombookstore.com/about-us/.
159. Teri French, Tulsa's Haunted Memories, (Charleston: Arcadia Publishing, 2010), 23–24.
160. "Peace of Mind Books," Facebook, https://www.facebook.com/PeaceOfMindBooks/info.
161. Peace of Mind Books, "About Peace of Mind Books," http://pombookstore.com/about-us/.
162. George Eberhart, "Library Ghosts; Northeastern U.S.," Encyclopedia Britannica Blog, http://www.britannica.com/blogs/2008/10/library-ghosts-northeastern-us/.
163. Michael A. Golrick, "A Library Ghost Story," Thoughts from a Library Administrator (blog), February 24, 2006, http://michaelgolrick.blogspot.com/2006/02/library-ghost-story.html.
164. "About Bridgeport Public Library," Bridgeport Library, http://bportlibrary.org/about/.
165. "The History of the Bridgeport Public Library," Bridgeport Library, http://bportlibrary.org/about/history/.
166. Ibid.
167. Ibid.
168. Nathaniel Hawthorne, The Ghost of Doctor Harris (New York: Tucker Publishing, 1900).
169. Brian Hicks, "Check out library's ghosts/spirit/presence," Post and Courier, October 31, 2007.
170. Ibid.
171. Ibid.
172. Ibid.
173. Ibid.
174. Ibid.
175. Ibid.
176. Ibid.

177. "History of the Library Society," Charleston Library Society, *http://www.charlestonlibrarysociety.org/index.html*.

178. Stephanie E. McCarthy, *Haunted Peoria* (Chicago: Arcadia Publishing, 2009), 43.

179. Ibid.

180. Stephanie E. McCarthy, *Haunted Peoria* (Chicago: Arcadia Publishing, 2009), 45.

181. Ibid.

182. Ibid.

183. "Haunted Libraries: Peoria Public Library," *The Witching Hour* (blog), *http://4girlsandaghost.wordpress.com/2014/01/03/haunted-libraries-peoria-public-library/*.

184. Stephanie E. McCarthy, *Haunted Peoria* (Chicago: Arcadia Publishing, 2009), 45.

185. Ibid.

186. Ibid.

187. Ibid.

188. Stephanie E. McCarthy, *Haunted Peoria* (Chicago: Arcadia Publishing, 2009), 46.

189. Ibid.

190. Ibid.

191. Ibid.

192. "History of the Library," Peoria Public Library, *http://www.peoriapubliclibrary.org/peoria-public-library-history*.

193. Ibid.

194. Illinois State Historical Society (1915), "Erastus S. Willcox," *Journal of the Illinois State Historical Society* (8:1), 198–201.

195. "History of the Library," Peoria Public Library, *http://www.peoriapubliclibrary.org/peoria-public-library-history*.

196. Illinois State Historical Society (1915), "Erastus S. Willcox," *Journal of the Illinois State Historical Society* (8:1), 198–201.

197. Stephanie E. McCarthy, *Haunted Peoria* (Chicago: Arcadia Publishing, 2009), 48.

198. Ibid.

199. Ibid.

200. Ibid.

201. Stephanie E. McCarthy, *Haunted Peoria* (Chicago: Arcadia Publishing, 2009), 50.

202. John B. Kachuba, *Ghosthunting Illinois* (Cincinnati, OH: Clerisy Press, 2005), 136.

203. John B. Kachuba, *Ghosthunting Illinois* (Cincinnati, OH: Clerisy Press, 2005), 137.

204. Ibid.

205. Stephanie E. McCarthy, *Haunted Peoria* (Chicago: Arcadia Publishing, 2009), 50.

206. Carolyn Kellogg, "Glendale Library haunted by Leslie Coombs Brand," *Los Angeles Times*, October 30, 2008.

207. Nancy Garza, "Something Ghostly This Way Comes," *Glendale News Press*, October 30, 1993, reprinted December 7, 2010, *http://www.brandlibrary.org/ghost.asp*.

208. Ibid.

209. Ibid.

210. Ibid.

211. Ibid.

212. Ibid.

213. Ibid.

214. Ibid.

215. Ibid.

216. Ibid.

217. "Pyramid Mausoleums," *Weird California*, http://www.weirdca. com/location.php?location=204.

218. "The History of the Brand Library," Brand Library, http:// www.brandlibrary.org/brand_ history.asp.

219. Kendyl Young, "History of Brant Park, Glendale — Part 1," *Glendale and Beyond*, http://glendaleandbeyond.com/ northwest-glendale/history-of- brand-park-glendale-part-1.

220. "The History of the Brand Library," Brand Library, http:// www.brandlibrary.org/brand_ history.asp.

221. David Martin, "A walk through the haunted library with those who know," *Green River Star*, October 26, 2011.

222. Dina Mishev, *Wyoming Curiosities* (New York: Guilford Press, 2007), 9.

223. Ibid, 8.

224. "Ghost Log Entries," *High Spirits: The Ghost Log Blog* (blog), Sweetwater County Library, http:// sweetwaterlibraries.com/sclsblogs/ ghostblog/?page_id=17.

225. David Martin, "A walk through the haunted library with those who know," *Green River Star*, October 26, 2011.

226. Ibid.

227. Dina Mishev, *Wyoming Curiosities* (New York: Guilford Press, 2007), 9.

228. Debra D. Munn, *Ghosts on the Range: Eerie True Tales of Wyoming* (Boulder, CO: Pruett Publishing, 1989), 87.

229. Ibid.

230. Ibid.

231. Debra D. Munn, *Ghosts on the Range: Eerie True Tales of Wyoming* (Boulder, CO: Pruett Publishing, 1989), 88.

232. Ibid.

233. Dina Mishev, *Wyoming Curiosities* (New York: Guilford Press, 2007), 9.

234. Debra D. Munn, *Ghosts on the Range: Eerie True Tales of Wyoming* (Boulder, CO: Pruett Publishing, 1989), 88.

235. Ibid.

236. Ibid.

237. Ibid, 89.

238. Ibid.

239. Ibid.

240. Ibid.

241. Ibid.

242. Ibid, 87.

243. Ibid, 89.

244. Ibid.

245. Judy Williams, "Ida Day returns to Hutch," *Hutchison News*, October 31, 1975.

246. Ibid.

247. Ibid.

248. Ibid.

249. Ibid.

250. Ibid.

251. Ibid.

252. Ibid.

253. Ibid.

254. Rich Newman, *The Ghost*

Hunters Field Guide (Woodbury, MN: Llewellyn, 2011), 109.

255. "An Historical Sketch," Hutchinson Public Library, http://www.hutchpl.org/images/first%20hpl%20historical%20booklet.pdf.

256. "About the Library," Hutchinson Public Library, http://www.hutchpl.org/overview/about-the-library.

257. Charlotte Sanchez-Kosa, "Ghost in bookstore likes to tease patrons," *Placerville Mountain Democrat*, October 27, 2010.

258. "Hidden Passage," California Haunts, http://www.californiahaunts.org/hidden.html.

259. Ibid.

260. Krysten Kellem, "Haunted Bookstore," *Placerville Mountain Democrat*, October 26, 2007.

261. Charlotte Sanchez-Kosa, "Ghost in bookstore likes to tease patrons," *Placerville Mountain Democrat*, October 27, 2010.

262. Krysten Kellem, "Haunted Bookstore," *Placerville Mountain Democrat*, October 26, 2007.

263. Ibid.

264. Ibid.

265. Ibid.

266. Charlotte Sanchez-Kosa, "Ghost in bookstore likes to tease patrons," *Placerville Mountain Democrat*, October 27, 2010.

267. Ibid.

268. Nancy Bradley, "Psychic Uncovers Ghost in a Book Store," *True Ghost Tales*, http://www.trueghosttales.com/paranormal/psychic-uncovers-ghosts-in-a-book-store/.

269. Ibid.

270. Ibid.

271. Ibid.

272. Ibid.

273. Tim Weisberg, *Ghosts of the SouthCoast* (Charleston: The History Press, 2008), 51.

274. Ibid.

275. Ibid.

276. Rebecca Aubet, "Fact of Fiction? The Search for the Truth Behind Fairhaven's Haunted Library," *South Coast Today*, October 26, 2005.

277. Tim Weisberg, *Ghosts of the SouthCoast*, (Charleston: The History Press, 2008), 51–52.

278. Rebecca Aubet, "Fact of Fiction? The Search for the Truth Behind Fairhaven's Haunted Library," *South Coast Today*, October 26, 2005.

279. Tim Weisberg, *Ghosts of the SouthCoast*, (Charleston: The History Press, 2008), 52.

280. "Fairhaven, Massachusetts Ghost Sightings," *Ghosts of America*, http://www.ghostsofamerica.com/0/Massachusetts_Fairhaven_ghost_sightings.html.

281. Tim Weisberg, *Ghosts of the SouthCoast*, (Charleston: The History Press, 2008), 52.

282. Rebecca Aubet, "Fact of Fiction? The Search for the Truth Behind Fairhaven's Haunted Library," *South Coast Today*, October 26, 2005.

283. Tim Weisberg, *Ghosts of the SouthCoast* (Charleston: The History Press, 2008), 54.

284. Tim Weisberg, "On a trip to Millicent, hauntings are recorded," *South Coast Today*, October 30, 2005.

285. Ibid.

286. Ibid.

287. Tim Weisberg, *Ghosts of the SouthCoast* (Charleston: The History Press, 2008), 50.

288. "Mark Twain and Henry Huddleston Rogers," The Millicent Library, *http://millicentlibrary.org/mark-twain-and-henry-huttleston-rogers/*.

289. Alan Brown, *Haunted Meridian, Mississippi* (Charleston: The Haunted Press, 2011), 67.

290. Jennifer Jacob, "Haunted places of East Mississippi and West Alabama," *Meridian Star*, October 20, 2008.

291. Alan Brown, *Haunted Meridian, Mississippi* (Charleston: The Haunted Press, 2011), 67.

292. "Book Returned 33 Years Late," *Biloxi Daily Herald*, March 16, 1961.

293. Jennifer Jacob, "Haunted places of East Mississippi and West Alabama," *Meridian Star*, October 20, 2008.

294. Ibid.

295. Jennifer Jacob, "Haunted places of East Mississippi and West Alabama," *Meridian Star*, October 20, 2008.

296. Alan Brown, *Haunted Meridian, Mississippi* (Charleston: The Haunted Press, 2011), 67.

297. Ibid.

298. Jennifer Jacob, "Haunted places of East Mississippi and West Alabama," *Meridian Star*, October 20, 2008.

299. Ibid.

300. Alan Brown, *Haunted Meridian, Mississippi* (Charleston: The Haunted Press, 2011), 66.

301. Jennifer Jacob, "Haunted places of East Mississippi and West Alabama," *Meridian Star*, October 20, 2008.

302. Ibid.

303. Ibid.

304. Ibid.

305. Ibid..

306. Ibid, 68–69.

307. Ibid, 67, 68.

308. Ibid, 68.

309. Ibid.

310. Karen Stevens, "Parmly Billings Library," *Haunted Montana* (blog), *http://www.hauntedmontana.com/index.php?p=1_50_February-2013*.

311. Greg Lamotte, "Haunted Building in Billings," *Chick Geek* (blog), March 7, 2013. *http://chickgeek.org/haunted-building-in-billings/*.

312. Ibid.

313. Ibid.

314. Jim Curry, "Parmly Billings Library: The First Hundred Years," Billings Public Library, *http://ci.billings.mt.us/DocumentCenter/Home/View/1843*.

315. "The new Billings Public Library is open and ready to welcome you!," Billings Public Library, http://ci.billings.mt.us/index.aspx?nid=1639.

316. Daniel Diel and Mark Donnelly, *Haunted Houses: Guide to Spooky, Creepy and Strange Places Across the USA* (Mechanicsburg, PA: Stackpole Books, 2010), 32–33.

317. Daniel Diel and Mark Donnelly, *Haunted Houses: Guide to Spooky, Creepy and Strange Places Across the USA* (Mechanicsburg, PA: Stackpole Books, 2010), 33.

318. Patricia A. Martinelli and Charles A. Stansfield, Jr., *The Big Book of New Jersey Ghost Stories*, (Mechanicsburg, PA: Stackpole Books, 2013), 127.

319. Ibid.

320. Laura Hladik, *Ghosthunting New Jersey* (Cincinnati: Clerisy Press, 2008), 125.

321. Patricia A. Martinelli and Charles A. Stansfield, Jr., *The Big Book of New Jersey Ghost Stories* (Mechanicsburg, PA: Stackpole Books, 2013), 127.

322. Laura Hladik, *Ghosthunting New Jersey* (Cincinnati: Clerisy Press, 2008), 125.

323. Ibid, 126.

324. Ibid.

325. Ibid, 126–27.

326. Patricia A. Martinelli and Charles A. Stansfield, Jr., *The Big Book of New Jersey Ghost Stories* (Mechanicsburg, PA: Stackpole Books, 2013), 128.

327. Dennis William Hauck, *Haunted Places; The National Directory* (New York: Penguin Books, 1994), 273.

328. Patricia A. Martinelli and Charles A. Stansfield, Jr., *The Big Book of New Jersey Ghost Stories* (Mechanicsburg, PA:

Stackpole Books, 2013), 128.

329. SA McNally, "The Ghost of Bernardsville Library," *Cryptoville* (blog), http://visitcryptoville.com/2013/11/27/the-ghost-of-bernardsville-library/.

330. Randolph Liebeck, "Bernardsville Library Ghost," *FATE Magazine*, October 1996.

331. George Eberhart, "Haunted Libraries in the U.S.: Nebraska — Oregon," *Encyclopaedia Britannica Blog*, http://www.britannica.com/blogs/2007/10/haunted-libraries-in-the-us-nebraska-oregon/.

332. Amy Baratta, "Ghost hunt: Old Bernardsville library stirs with spirits," *Bernardsville News*, July 22, 2011.

333. Ibid.

334. Ibid.

International

1. "About Windsor Castle," Royal Collection Trust, http://www.royalcollection.org.uk/visit/windsorcastle/about.

2. Ibid.

3. Patrick Bernauw, "The ghost of Anne Boleyn," *Unexplained Mysteries*, June 9, 2009, http://www.unexplained-mysteries.com/column.php?id=155702.

4. Ghostly Admin, "Ghosts of Windsor Castle. Berkshire," *Haunted Island* (blog), http://www.hauntedisland.co.uk/famous-hauntings/ghosts-of-windsor-castle-berkshire.

5. Jacky Newcomb, *Heaven* (London: Penguin Books,

2013), 128.

6. Ibid.

7. Ghostly Admin, "Ghosts of Windsor Castle. Berkshire," *Haunted Island* (blog), *http://www.hauntedisland.co.uk/famous-hauntings/ghosts-of-windsor-castle-berkshire.*

8. David and Charles Editors, *Tales of Haunted Places* (Cincinnati: F+W Media, 2010).

9. Ghostly Admin, "Ghosts of Windsor Castle. Berkshire," *Haunted Island* (blog), *http://www.hauntedisland.co.uk/famous-hauntings/ghosts-of-windsor-castle-berkshire.*

10. "Windsor Castle," Delco Ghosts, http://www.delcoghosts.com/windsor.html.

11. "About us," Sarah Key Books / The Haunted Bookshop, *http://www.sarahkeybooks.co.uk/about/.*

12. Ibid.

13. Emilie Ferris, "The Haunted Bookshop," *The Tab*, January 22, 2011, *http://cambridge.tab.co.uk/2011/01/22/the-haunted-bookshop/.*

14. Ibid.

15. Ibid.

16. "History," Combermere Abbey, *http://www.combermereabbey.co.uk/the-abbey/history.*

17. Ibid.

18. "Ghosts and the Paranormal," Combermere Abbey, *http://www.combermereabbey.co.uk/the-abbey/ghosts-and-paranormal.*

19. "Combermere Abbey," *Wikipedia, http://en.wikipedia.*

org/wiki/Combermere_Abbey.

20. Jason Karl, *An Illustrated History of the Haunted World*, (London: New Holland Publishers, 2007), 87.

21. Ibid.

22. "Ghosts and the Paranormal," Combermere Abbey, *http://www.combermereabbey.co.uk/the-abbey/ghosts-and-paranormal.*

23. Ibid.

24. William F. Barrett, *On The Threshold of the Unseen*, (New York: E.P. Dutton & Company, 1918), 90–91.

25. "Leeds Central Library," *Wikipedia, http://en.wikipedia.org/wiki/Leeds_Central_Library.*

26. "Preview: Ghost Hunting at Leeds Central Library," *Leeds-List.com*, February 21, 2013, *http://leeds-list.com/out-and-about/preview-ghost-hunting-at-leeds-central-library/.*

27. Ibid.

28. Ibid.

29. "Ghost Hunt with Pontefract Paranormal," *Skiddle*, http://www.skiddle.com/whats-on/Leeds/Leeds-Central-Library/Ghost-Hunt-with-Pontefract-Paranormal/11872874/.

30. Ibid.

31. "Leeds Central Library," *Wikipedia, http://en.wikipedia.org/wiki/Leeds_Central_Library.*

32. "Central Library," Leeds City Council, *http://www.leeds.gov.uk/leisure/Pages/Central-library.aspx.*

33. "Librarians of the Leeds Library," The Leeds Library,

http://www.theleedslibrary.org.
uk/about-us/history/people/
librarians/list-of-librarians.

34. Richard Smyth, *Bloody British History: Leeds* (Stroud, UK: The History Press, 2013), 87.
35. Ibid.
36. Richard Smyth, *Bloody British History: Leeds* (Stroud, UK: The History Press, 2013), 87–88.
37. Ibid, 88.
38. Ibid.
39. Ibid.
40. Ibid, 89.
41. Ibid.
42. Ibid.
43. Ibid.
44. Ibid, 90.
45. John Winchurch, "Vincent Thomas Sternberg and the haunting of Leeds Library," *John Winchurch pictures* (blog), http://jonvicpics.wordpress.com/2009/06/01/vincent-thomas-sternberg-and-the-haunting-of-leeds-library/.
46. "About us," The Leeds Library, http://www.theleedslibrary.org.uk/about-us.
47. "Leeds Library," *Wikipedia*, http://en.wikipedia.org/wiki/Leeds_Library.
48. "Collections," The Leeds Library, http://www.theleedslibrary.org.uk/collections.
49. "The Hall," Felbrigg Hall Gardens and Estate, http://www.nationaltrust.org.uk/felbrigg-hall/things-to-see-and-do/the-hall/.
50. Lenora Jessel, "The Ghosts of Felbrigg Hall," *The Haunted Palace* (blog), April 17, 2013,

http://hauntedpalaceblog.wordpress.com/2013/04/17/the-ghosts-of-felbrigg-hall/.
51. Ibid.
52. Ibid.
53. "William Windham," *Wikipedia*, http://en.wikipedia.org/wiki/William_Windham.
54. George Eberhart, "Haunted Libraries Around the World: Europe, Asia, Australia, Mexico," *Encyclopedia Britannica Blog*, October 24, 2007, http://www.britannica.com/blogs/2007/10/haunted-libraries-around-the-world-europe-asia-australia-mexico/.
55. Ibid.
56. "Felbrigg Hall," *Wikipedia*, http://en.wikipedia.org/wiki/Felbrigg_Hall.
57. "The Hall," Felbrigg Hall Gardens and Estate, http://www.nationaltrust.org.uk/felbrigg-hall/things-to-see-and-do/the-hall/.
58. Ibid.
59. "England's Haunted Arundel Castle," Fringe Paranormal, July 29, 2011, http://fringeparanormal.wordpress.com/2011/07/29/englands-haunted-arundel-castle/.
60. Ibid.
61. Ibid.
62. Charles A. Coulombe, *Haunted Castles of the World* (New York: Globe Pequot Press, 2004), 23.
63. Rosemary Ellen Guiley, *Encyclopedia of Ghosts and Spirits* (New York: Facts on File, 1992), 20.
64. Isebel Dunstan, "State Library of Victoria," *Time Out*

Melbourne, November 19, 2010, *http://www.au.timeout.com/ melbourne/museums/venues/24/ state-library-of-victoria.*

65. "Library Ghouls," *Intelligent Travel Blog*, National Geographic, October 31, 2007, *http://intelligenttravel. nationalgeographic. com/2007/10/31/library_ghouls/.*

66. Ibid.

67. "History of the Library," State Library of Victoria, *http://www. slv.vic.gov.au/about-us/history-library.*

68. "Our Vision," State Library of Victoria, *http://www.slv.vic.gov. au/about-us/our-vision.*

69. The Haunted Bookshop, http:// *www.haunted.com.au/contents. html#reviews.*

70. Tim Richards, "Things That Go Bump in the Night," *Jetstar Magazine*, October 2008, 43.

71. Ibid.

72. The Haunted Bookshop, http:// *www.haunted.com.au/news/ upstart.html.*

73. "History," Marsh's Library, *http://www.marshlibrary.ie/ history/.*

74. David H. Stam, *International Dictionary of Library Histories* (Chicago: Fitzroy Dearborn Publishers, 2001), 195.

75. Ibid.

76. Ibid.

77. John Dunne, *A Ghost Watcher's Guide to Ireland* (Louisiana: Appletree Press, 2001), 48.

78. "About Nacissis Marsh," Marsh's Library, *http://www. marshlibrary.ie/about/narcissus-*

marsh/.

79. Ibid.

80. John Dunne, *A Ghost Watcher's Guide to Ireland* (Louisiana: Appletree Press, 2001), 48.

81. Marsh's Library, *http://www. marshlibrary.ie/.*

82. "Welcome to Rammerscales," Rammerscales, *http://www. rammerscales.co.uk/.*

83. Christopher Winn, *Things I Never Knew About the Scottish* (London: Ebury Publishing, 2009).

84. George M. Eberhart, *The Whole Library Handbook 4* (New York: American Library Association, 2006), 572.

85. "Brodick Castle," Glasgow Paranormal Investigators, *http://www.thegpi.co.uk/?p=369.*

86. Ibid.

87. George White, *Ghost Stories from the North of England*, e-book, 2013. According to a note by author George White in the beginning of this electronic-only book, "The contents of this book are the combined works contained in five pamphlets published between 1972 and 1982 by Rebecca Dain and Craig McNeil. These pamphlets have been out of print for some thirty years and this is in itself a minor calamity as it has deprived paranormal researchers (and not to mention lovers of ghost yarns) of good source books for special phenomena in the North of England. Hopefully this compilation will correct this lacuna."

88. "Attractions in Morelia, Mexico," *BestDay, http://www.bestday.com/Morelia_Michoacan/Attractions/.*

89. Scott Corrales, "Darkness Abides: A Tour of Haunted Structures", *Inexplicata — The Journal of Hispanic Ufology* (blog), *http://inexplicata.blogspot.ca/2013/01/darkness-abides-tour-of-haunted.html.*

90. Ibid.

91. Ibid.

92. Ibid.

93. "Kimberly and its ghosts," Road Travel Africa, Sept 14, 2011, *http://roadtravelafrica.com/2011/09/14/kimberley-and-its-ghosts/.*

94. Ibid.

95. Ibid.

96. Ibid.

97. "Kimberly's ghost tours," South Africa Tourism, *http://www.southafrica.net/za/en/articles/entry/article-southafrica.net-the-kimberley-ghost-tour.*

98. Africana Library, *http://www.africanalibrary.co.za/.*

99. Ibid.

100. Ibid.

101. "Kimberly and its ghosts," Road Travel Africa, Sept 14, 2011, *http://roadtravelafrica.com/2011/09/14/kimberley-and-its-ghosts/.*

102. Samuel P. Jacobs, "The Skinny on Harvard's Rare Book Collection," *Harvard Crimson*, February 2, 2006, *http://www.thecrimson.com/article/2006/2/2/the-skinny-on-harvards-rare-book/.*

103. Ibid.

104. Ibid.

105. Ibid.

106. Ibid.

107. Daniel Lovering, "'Human skin' book at Harvard found to be bound in sheepskin," *Reuters*, April 4, 2014, *http://www.reuters.com/article/2014/04/04/us-usa-skin-harvard-idUSBREA331VF20140404.*

108. Samuel P. Jacobs, "The Skinny on Harvard's Rare Book Collection," *Harvard Crimson*, February 2, 2006, *http://www.thecrimson.com/article/2006/2/2/the-skinny-on-harvards-rare-book/.*

109. Lindsey Fitzharris, "Books of Human Flesh: The History behind Anthropodermic Bibliopegy," *The Chirurgeon's Apprentice* (blog), Jan 31, 2012, *http://thechirurgeonsapprentice.com/2012/01/31/books-of-human-flesh-the-history-behind-anthropodermic-bibliopegy/#f1.*

110. Annetta Black, "A morbid secret lies within the beautiful walls of the Boston Anthanaeum," *Atlas Obscura,* retrieved April 2, 2014, *http://www.atlasobscura.com/places/boston-athenaeum.*

Appendices

1. George Eberhart, "Haunted Libraries Around the World: The Complete List," *Encyclopaedia Britannica Blog*, October 31, 2007, *http://www.britannica.com/blogs/2007/10/haunted-libraries-around-the-world-the-complete-list/.*